SELECTED POEMS OF

JOHN DRYDEN

Edited with an Introduction and Notes

by

ROGER SHARROCK

HEINEMANN

LONDON

Heinemann Educational Books Ltd

LONDON MELBOURNE TORONTO
SINGAPORE JOHANNESBURG
HONG KONG NAIROBI
AUCKLAND IBADAN

SBN   435 15032 4 (cased edition)
        435 15033 2 (paperback)

JOHN DRYDEN 1631-1700

INTRODUCTION AND NOTES
© ROGER SHARROCK 1963, 1968

FIRST PUBLISHED 1963
REPRINTED 1964, 1966,
SECOND EDITION 1968

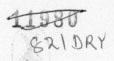
Published by
Heinemann Educational Books Ltd
48 Charles Street, London W.1
Printed in Great Britain by Morrison and Gibb Ltd
London and Edinburgh

CONTENTS

NOTE TO SECOND EDITION

In this edition an extract from *Absalom and Achitophel*, Part Two (ll. 310–509), has been added to the selection, together with relevant notes, and small additions to the Introduction and Bibliography.

JOHN DRYDEN
(*artist unknown*)

SELECTED POEMS OF
JOHN DRYDEN

THE POETRY BOOKSHELF

General Editor: James Reeves

INTRODUCTION

I

ON 25 May 1660 Charles II landed at Dover to be greeted on
the shore by General Monk and an enthusiastic concourse of
people, 'blackening all the strand', as Dryden was later to write.
'All things very gallant and joyful', said Pepys, who observed
the scene from a boat which he shared with a member of the
royal household engaged to look after one of the King's spaniels.
Four days later Charles entered London amid scenes of even
greater joy, and this was followed by the pageantry of his
coronation which deliberately stressed the renewal of national
prosperity and power to be expected from a restored monarchy.
A new age was proclaimed: the eighteenth century, when we
speak of it as a term in cultural history, to describe a state of
mind associated with a certain moment of civilization, began
for England in 1660.

It was a new age very conscious of its newness, aware of the
gulf that divided it from the past and deliberately experimental
in the methods it employed to mark out its own special character.
The Elizabethans had been proud of their country's achieve-
ments; as patriots they honoured the greatness of their queen,
and as men of the Renaissance they cherished a high ideal of the
renown due to the poet and artist. But the Restoration mind
possessed the rudiments of an historical sense; it saw 'the last
age' (the Elizabethan period) as different, antiquated in its ideas
slightly barbarous in its manners, and, though marvellously
energetic in its use of the English language, crude and immature
The new age cultivated a polish and a sense of form that had
not been known before in all the arts of communication; it was
really a sense of manners converted into a sense of style. Words
and phrases were taught to behave with ease and social propriety

as the proper instruments of a gentleman in polite society. Dryden was to declare, in his *Epilogue to the Second Part of the Conquest of Granada*,

> Wit's now arriv'd to a more high degree;
> Our native Language more refin'd and free;
> Our ladies and our men now speak more wit
> In conversation, than those Poets writ.

At the same time the exploitation of recent inventions like the magnetic compass widened the gulf between thoughtful late seventeenth-century Englishmen and the immediate past; increased trade had brought a new and more luxurious style of living to London, transforming the social life of the capital. For a few of the reasons of which we today have so many more a man of the Restoration could appreciate the special flavour of modernity and see himself fixed in the present, a creature of its particular modes. The resemblance would end there, however, since things were not changing rapidly enough for the Restoration writer or man of fashion to develop that sense of flux, of one present bewilderingly succeeding another, that has been the lot of the last half-century.

However, the sense of being at the beginning of a new age was tempered by caution and a fear of extremes; it was a post-war period; England was licking its wounds after the upheaval of the Civil Wars and Interregnum: Charles II admitted that a wish not to go upon his travels again was the mainspring of his policy, and the majority of his countrymen followed him in being ruled by the desire to pursue their private concerns in peace. The great absolutes that had governed men's minds during the English Revolution and seemed worth the sacrifice of their lives and fortunes were looked at coolly and critically. Passionate adherence to a cause was at a discount, for it was such passion that had sent Cromwell's Ironsides into battle singing the 68th Psalm, 'Let God arise and let his enemies be scattered', that had sent the King's father to the block, and had tried by the imposition of military rule to see that there should be no more

2

cakes and ale. Nor were the high courtesies of the chivalrous imagination any more respected; they had, after all, been ineffectual: a Falkland and a Montrose had died while intriguers and time-servers had survived. 'Enthusiasm' and 'enthusiast' were terms of opprobrium; they were used to describe the fanatics of the extreme Puritan sects who claimed a private revelation of divine grace. The anarchic individualism of the sectaries had provided the motive power to divide the Parliamentary cause against itself and to prolong the conflict. It was little wonder that some of the slur now attached to 'enthusiastic' notions was communicated to other forms of passionate imagination where claim was laid to the test of inspiration or individual authenticity, whether in poetry or art or philosophical speculation.

Distrust of the irrational and the attempt to see the world soberly in the light of sense experience are primary elements in the teaching of Hobbes, who, if he was the bogey man of the age because of his reputed atheism, was also, until Locke's *Essay* was published at the end of the century, its most influential philosopher. He states as arguments many ideas which became the unconscious presuppositions of the period. Among them were disrespect for the mere authority of the ancients as such in any discipline (this was a major departure from the slavish traditionalism of the high Renaissance which aspired no further than to rediscover the pure word of Greece and Rome, whether on the rules of the drama, on architecture or philosophy); the attack on mystery and inspiration based on a materialistic psychology; and, running throughout his thought, the attempt to reduce abstractions and complexes of emotion to clear and simple ideas. Thus the fantastic creatures that people our dreams, and *mutatis mutandis* our mythologies and the dreams of the poets, occur when the judgment is suspended and the ideas of sense (i.e. the images derived from our sense impressions) become arbitrarily linked together: we confuse the idea of a horse and the idea of a man and create a centaur. According to

3

this way of thinking, poetic myth, whether in a large conception like *The Faerie Queene* or in the passionate dialectic of a metaphysical lyric, is seen not as the fine flower of the mind but as something executed when the superior part of the intellect is asleep, and therefore primitive or slightly childish. It is no wonder that in poetry of the age after Hobbes imagery, when it is not the fruit of careful observation, is apt to be merely decorative; and the handling of classical mythology, so vital in poets of the early Renaissance, becomes a painted backcloth: myth turns into personification.

Older truths might be called in question, but the new philosophy welcomed the evidence of the senses and made possible the discovery of a new realm by the experimental scientists, and the eventual establishment, by Newton and Locke, of a new picture of the world. The Royal Society, under the patronage of the King and the court, enjoyed great prestige; Dryden was one of its early members. It helped to create an efficient prose style, an instrument of precise reference in which experiments could be described so that all men should understand them, the 'close, naked, natural way of speaking' mentioned by Sprat, the Society's first historian. Something of the reasoned clarity of this scientists' prose, together with their unscientific and often quite enthusiastic appetite for natural marvels, rubbed off upon the poets. The reasonable apprehension of the wonders of nature was something that remained the same for all men, and the sceptical bent of the post-Restoration period tended to believe that if truth were to be found it must be universally communicable.

A predominant body of thought in the Church of England was ready to found the arguments for the Christian religion on the same principle—the common ground of reason in the minds of all men. Preachers and writers who would have been shocked to agree with Hobbes, or to find themselves confused with the Deists, preferred nevertheless to base their arguments on natural religion. Moral exhortation was now conducted from an appeal to common decencies instead of supernatural sanctions. Scholastic doctrines and cumbersome catalogues of authorities disappeared from the sermon, and what took their place was a clear, reasonable argument expressed in a polished version of the colloquial language of the day.

In church and state the spirit of compromise was at work. Peace and social order demanded a reconciliation of all those conflicting interests that for twenty years had torn the community apart. In 1662 the Puritan ministers were ejected from their livings; some of them and most of the Quakers were cruelly persecuted from time to time; the Catholics suffered during the scare of the Popish Plot in 1678-9; but the main reason for the sporadic ill-treatment of these minorities was the belief, rightly or wrongly held, that their behaviour endangered, not the souls of their fellow countrymen, but the secular prosperity and security of the state. After the great clash of opposites Dryden and his contemporaries were aware of different points of view, sceptically concerned in maintaining a due balance between arguments that often seemed irreconcilable. It was in the Restoration period that the English political compromise was worked out; it did not spring from the legalism of the Long Parliament, or the pure democracy of the Army Debates, or from the complete Whig victory of 1688.

II

John Dryden is the greatest poet of this age, and the first great English man of letters, a writer earning his living as dramatist, translator, controversialist and critic, as well as poet, and at the same time actively concerned with the health and standards of every branch of literature which he touched. He is usually coupled with Pope, he as the founder, Pope as the perfecter of the English neo-classical school of poetry; he certainly belongs to that larger eighteenth century; he was the pioneer of a new music in verse and a new exclusiveness in vocabulary; but he is also especially associated with those

5

features of the Restoration age itself which were not perpetuated when the national compromise was fully worked out and things had settled down. Like the outrageous Hobbist courtiers who were his friends he is used to a sceptical atmosphere in which the argument is carried as far as it will go. Like them he can see the enemy's case and give him the benefit of the doubt.

Old enough to have grown up during the war and the Commonwealth, he was exposed to Puritan influences in his youth and as a young man was a moderate supporter of the Commonwealth. Then he passed from a phase which may be described as pure 'libertine' scepticism, through High Anglicanism, to a final submission to the Roman Church. In this passage, he was able to put to the test the standards approved by contemporary opinion. While never abandoning the method of close argument and careful discrimination, he grew suspicious of the claims of reason to be the sole passport to truth. In this he was like many of his contemporaries: Rochester, courtier, profligate and poet, converted on his deathbed, is another distinguished example. There is always a scepticism which clears away the rubble of assumptions only to find a new resting place by deifying reason, and another kind concerned to journey sceptically on rather than to arrive, and which, if in the end it finds resting places for the human spirit, does not attempt to justify them in terms of the unaided human reason. Dryden's scepticism was of the latter kind. He has too often been treated as a mere court poet, a versifier of party opinions. He is not, of course, a philosophical poet as Lucretius and Dante are: poets who have drawn from a particular metaphysical system the material to sustain a complex imaginative structure. But in the ambience of Hobbes and the Royal Society, and perhaps too of Montaigne and Pascal, how could he be? Yet he thinks in verse by being sturdily faithful to a certain method of dialectic, and finding the form to suit it, dialogue or fable or verse pamphlet, and a language to catch the tone of the market-place and the coffee-house from a little above them. Nowadays when we

6

have experienced our own Hobbist revolution and a cold wind has blown from Oxford and Cambridge alike on the inflated currencies of metaphysics and introspective poetry we shall perhaps not hesitate to describe Dryden's plain and patient mode of discourse as philosophic.

He is of the age too in a vein of coarse realism which ranges all the way from robust splendour in lampoon and narrative to the smut of his stage prologues and epilogues. Though he bears the chief responsibility for reforming and classicizing the language of poetry, his own language retains what Johnson, borrowing a term from viniculture, calls the *race*, the flavour of the soil. There is a largeness and freedom of movement in his poems, often a grand carelessness, which would have been out of place in the Augustan Age proper: they would have offended its stricter sense of decorum, just as his questing, travelling mind would not have accepted the settled complacency of eighteenth-century rationalism.

His family were landed gentry in Northamptonshire, and he was born in that county on 9 August 1631 at Aldwincle All Saints. He was educated at Westminster School under a famous headmaster, Dr Busby. All the poets of the Augustan period were taught Latin and Greek at public schools where the aim of the curriculum was to teach them to write like the classical authors, adopting a style suitable to the given theme. Horace and Quintilian were studied as a storehouse of instruments to be used in composition.

> Thus useful arms in magazines we place,
> All rang'd in order, and dispos'd with grace.[1]

When Dryden translated a satire of Persius in his old age he could write:

I remember I translated this Satyr, when I was a *Kings-Scholar* at *Westminster* School, for a *Thursday* Nights *Exercise*; and believe that it, and many other of my *Exercises* of this nature, in *English Verse*,

[1] Pope, *Essay on Criticism*, 672–3.

are still in the Hands of my *Learned Master*, the Reverend Doctor *Busby*.[1]

Original composition was only a step removed from such exercises and between it and translation there was no clear line of demarcation. Poets trained like this were bound to produce work that was professional and rhetorical in quality.

He proceeded to Trinity College, Cambridge, and took the bachelor's degree in January 1654. Shortly after that he settled in London to make his way by literature. He did not have to live by his pen; he had inherited a small estate on which he could have lived, and later his marriage brought him money and a valuable alliance with a noble family; he had his financial ups and downs and was often in need of money, but at another time he was in a strong enough position to make a loan to the King (he was lucky enough to be repaid). It was by temperament that he became a man of letters, and a serious interest in the different literary genres that impelled him to attempt so many. This fact is often ignored on account of the bulk of his commissioned works, their frequent topical reference, and the rewards from patrons which they inevitably elicited. But these were the ordinary conditions of literary work at the time. Dryden could not have poured out his soul in a retired cell; to him the poet *in his rôle as poet* was a social figure; it is more important to see that he could have been a witty trifler, idling out verses and epigrams as one of 'The mob of gentlemen who wrote with ease', if his craftsman's affections had not set him upon a different career.

At the height of his powers his command of verse was easy and masterful, but he took a long time, longer than most great English poets, to reach this mastery. Hardly any of his best work was produced before his fortieth year, very little before his fiftieth (with the important exception of *Macflecknoe* which was probably circulating in manuscript in 1678). He was a slow developer, but there is another reason for this delay. Between

[1] The Third Satire of Persius, note appended to the Argument.

8

1663 and 1681 he devoted a great part of his energy to the theatre. In terms of material success the total result was a drawn battle between Dryden and the stage: he never enjoyed an overwhelming popularity. There have been different views on the merits of his plays but no one has ever suggested that they occupy a high place in his work. With their monotonous points of honour and solo declamations, like operatic arias, plays like *The Conquest of Granada* remain period pieces; *All For Love*, Dryden's ingenious conversion of *Antony and Cleopatra* to a Restoration heroic tragedy, has worn better than most. The comedies have intricately complicated plots, with combats in the new smart manner, the bright, emancipated treatment of adultery and the sex war; but not one of them is as good a play as the best comedies of Wycherley, or Etherege or Congreve. The lure of the stage is often the last infirmity of the poet or novelist, as Keats was tempted to begin a *King Stephen*, Tennyson to write a *Becket* and a *Queen Mary*, and Henry James to commit a *Guy Domville*. Dryden, however, reversed the usual process and spent the best years of his life in writing for the theatre; he was no closet dramatist, but was engaged in giving his public what it wanted, or, at any rate, in making it want what he had to give it. Rehearsals had to be attended; then there were the incessant controversies on topical questions (for instance, rhyme against blank verse), personal quarrels, and rivalries, and the financial crises of the different theatre companies. Such an apprenticeship left Dryden nearly as jaded by the popular theatre as Ben Jonson had been at the end of his career. It left him too with few illusions about human nature, and an attitude to verse that saw it as a social tool, an element in the rhetorical game of expressing or defining or denouncing a given attitude within the small group in which he moved. Above all, from adapting it to the ears of his audience in a dozen plays he learned just what could be done with the heroic couplet, the metre of Chaucer's tales, of *Hero and Leander*, and of most English translations of classical poems in the hexameter at that time.

III

When Waller and Denham were engaged in reforming versification and introducing a needed clarity into expression, Dryden was beginning his career with poetry in the rugged metre and tortuous manner of the decadent metaphysical school. His earliest poem, *Upon the Death of the Lord Hastings*, contains the extravagant conceit

> Each little pimple had a tear in it
> To wail the fault its rising did commit.

(Hastings had died of smallpox.) But this is juvenile work and simply shows that Dryden lived before the revolution he helped to make, and that from the start he tried what could be done with any style, seeking out the effects it was best calculated to yield.

He may have held some minor post under the Commonwealth. On the death of Cromwell in 1658 he wrote *Heroic Stanzas* to his memory, and two years later he welcomed the returned King with *Astraea Redux* and another poem. This is faintly comic but hardly disgraceful: in the intervening period he had changed with the nation. He remained consistently loyal to the Stuart house and the idea of a limited but strong monarchy. He married in 1663 Lady Elizabeth Howard, daughter of Thomas, Earl of Berkshire. Rumour had it that the marriage was unhappy and there is evidence that for many years he kept a mistress, the actress Anne Reeve.

Dryden soon acquired powerful patrons and gained a footing among the wits of the court. He was interested in the new science and in current suggestions for the reform of the English language; he was a member of the Royal Society's committee on language. His work as a dramatist made him still better known to the small upper-class audience of the London theatres. Though a modern, ready to exploit the new, realistic appeal of the witty, amoral comedy of manners, he never lost a proper sense of the achievement of the older dramatists of the age of Shakespeare and Jonson; his chief contribution to comedy was the pair of witty, sparring lovers who fight out the sex war in so many Restoration comedies until Congreve brings them to perfection in the Mirabell and Millamant of *The Way of the World*. His *Essay of Dramatic Poesy* (1668) shows that liberal, cautious awareness of different possibilities that characterizes his critical outlook. It is in dialogue form, so that the strict French adherence to the unities of time and place, the loose English method of plotting, and other methods of construction, can each be argued on its own merits by a partisan. The participants in the dialogue have been identified with literary men of the time, but it is truer to the nature of Dryden's thought to see that this kind of dialogue was going on in his mind all the time.

His most ambitious poem before 1682 was *Annus Mirabilis* (1667), written to calm public fears after the Plague, the Great Fire of London, and the setbacks of the Second Dutch War. It is a heroic poem, exalting the achievements of Britain, its King, scientists, engineers, architects, and admirals. But though Dryden has Virgil in his mind his treatment is daringly modernistic, coining new words and introducing technical terms; even for this he has a classical precedent in Virgil's *Georgics*. In 1668 he was made Poet Laureate and in 1670 Historiographer-Royal. The next ten years were occupied with various literary disputes. After the success of *The Conquest of Granada*, his most important heroic play, he was ridiculed as 'Mr Bayes' by the Duke of Buckingham in his brilliant parody play *The Rehearsal* (1671). Dryden in his turn vigorously lampooned the dramatist Settle, and became estranged from Shadwell who had been his friend; the quarrel led to the composition of his first great satire *Macflecknoe*. He also quarrelled with the King's Company who had produced all his plays so far. He found time, however, to read widely in critical theory and to refine the bombastic diction and unreal characters of his heroic plays. He 'grew weary of his long-lov'd mistress, Rhyme', and in *All For Love* (1678) turned to blank verse. By study and practice, arguing the problem out preface by preface, he moved towards a classical simplicity of action. After *The Spanish Friar* (1680) he wrote little for the theatre.

After 1681, when he was over fifty, Dryden emerged in a few years as a satirical and didactic poet of the first stature. The first part of *Absalom and Achitophel* was published by Tonson at the end of that year; the second part, only portions of which were by Dryden, *The Medal, Religio Laici* and *Macflecknoe* all appeared in 1682. *The Hind and the Panther* was published in 1687. Dryden had now become a Catholic and in that poem he defends the claims of the Roman Church against the Anglican.

Dryden had been for several years a spokesman of the royal party; his conversion came soon after the accession of James II, a Catholic who attempted to impose Catholicism on court and country; it was inevitable that he should be accused of acting from self-interest. But in fact Dryden received no extra emolument or advantage as a result of his change of faith; on the contrary, at the Revolution when Protestantism was restored he lost all his official posts and endured some poverty but remained true to his profession. Johnson, critical of Dryden's Catholicism but just to his character, has said the last word on the matter:

> ... information may come at a commodious time ... when opinions are struggling into popularity, the arguments by which they are opposed or defended become more known; and he that changes his profession would perhaps have changed it before, with the like opportunities of instruction.[1]

There is plenty of evidence in the poems that Dryden had been gradually approaching a Catholic position. In *Religio Laici* his dialectic explores the contradictions of Protestant reliance on the authority of the Bible; here and elsewhere he shows too his distrust of mobs and majorities (and Anglicanism in England was a majority), and his search for a principle of authority not

[1] *Lives of the Poets,* 'Dryden'

subject to the human reason's capacity for self-deception. The fine confessional passage in *The Hind and the Panther* represents the full ripening of much previous experience rather than a new beginning:

> My thoughtless youth was wing'd with vain desires,
> My manhood, long misled by wand'ring fires,
> Follow'd false lights; and, when their glimpse was gone,
> My pride struck out new sparkles of her own.
> Such was I, such by nature still I am;
> Be thine the glory, and be mine the shame.

Dryden's last years were dogged by poverty and ill health but his mental vigour was undiminished. As well as a stream of occasional poems and critical essays he produced a series of magnificent translations from the Greek and Latin classics. Many of these are contained in four great miscellanies (the miscellaneous volume was becoming a favourite mode of poetic publication at this time). These are as follows: *Miscellany Poems* (1684), *Sylvae* (1685), *Examen Poeticum* (1693), and *The Annual Miscellany* (1694). To these should be added *The Satires of Juvenal and Persius Made English* (1693), and the masterpiece which completes the series, Dryden's version of the *Works of Virgil* (1697).

Though he was now writing to maintain himself, his last works were not commissioned tasks but loving exercises on the subjects most congenial to him, easy, rapid narratives and familiar epistles. His last collection, *Fables Ancient and Modern* (1700), contains his free translations from Boccaccio and adaptations of Chaucer into modern English. In this splendid Indian summer of his last poems Dryden reveals a close sympathy with Chaucer who had also based his poetry on good sense, had cared for the natural resources of the language, and had come to rest content with the field of men and manners as his most suitable subject. What he says of Chaucer in the preface tells us much of his own poetic character:

> He is the father of English poetry, so I hold him in the same degree

13

of veneration as the Grecians held Homer, or the Romans Virgil. He is a perpetual fountain of good sense, learn'd in all sciences; and, therefore, speaks properly on all subjects. As he knew what to say, so he knows also when to leave off; a continence which is practised by few writers, and scarcely by any of the ancients, excepting Virgil and Horace. . . .

Chaucer followed Nature everywhere, but was never so bold to go beyond her; and there is a great difference of being *poeta* and *nimis poeta*, if we may believe Catullus, as much as betwixt a modest behaviour and affectation.

He must have been a man of the most wonderful comprehensive nature, because, as it has been truly observed of him, he has taken into the compass of his *Canterbury Tales* the various manners and humours (as we now call them) of the whole English nation, in his age.

Dryden was short, plump and rosy-faced. He was retiring in society and did not talk with ease. Congreve and others speak of his kindness, modesty, and readiness to help young writers. In the last decade of his life he reigned over the wits from his chair in Will's Coffee-House. He had helped to call into being 'the town', that ever-flowing current of metropolitan taste and opinion which had hardly existed before his time; now the succession was to be handed on, first to Addison, then to Johnson and the Club, later to the quarterly reviewers. He had made the English literary mind conscious of itself, and it was to continue to be so, down to Bloomsbury and the *Criterion* and our own day.

IV

Dryden's reputation, like that of his successor Pope, was eclipsed during the romantic period and subsequently. Matthew Arnold, taking his stand on the doctrine of the poetic subject, declared them 'not classics of our poetry, but classics of our prose'; and elsewhere he said, 'their poetry is conceived and composed in their wits, genuine poetry is composed in the soul'. The nineteenth century tried to restrict poetry to the consoling subject and the elevated state of mind. When these restrictions were removed, Dryden returned to favour. The praise of Mark Van Doren and T. S. Eliot reverses the values of the nineteenth century by saluting Dryden precisely because he observes the limits of the sound craftsman, the journeyman of letters who sticks to his last. Poetry is made with words, not with high sentiments, and as Gerard Manley Hopkins said in the period when Dryden's merits were discounted, 'his style and his rhythms lay the strongest stress of all our literature on the naked thew and sinew of the English language'[1]; but his modern critics have been perhaps too concerned to present him as an object-lesson in the aberrations of romantic taste to study his positive qualities in detail.

The rehabilitation of Dryden as a major poet is thus apt to seem the work of literary politics rather than conviction. The modern reader, whether consciously or not, is usually guided by notions of what a poem should be which derive from symbolism. It should be, not do; it should not state something, but offer a unified experience not definable in any other terms, so that its operation may better be compared to that of a flower or a musical phrase or to a dance movement than to the non-poetic use of words in discourse. Dryden's poems emphatically do things; they point to purposes outside the poems, they make statements which can be paraphrased as political manifestos or logical arguments. And when he tells a plain tale in the *Fables* it is so plain that a new critic would be hard put to it to detect an 'intention' or an 'irony' any more remote than the worldly-wise serene humour arising from the events themselves.

We can, of course, fall back on a standard of craftsmanlike efficiency. We can say that his poems are jobs well done, not flowers with a unique inner being, but perfectly adjusted to their functions like a good pot or pan or certain modern buildings. This would be drab, and true, but would still leave nine-tenths unsaid about the permanent strength of his poetry and the delight

The Letters of Gerard Manley Hopkins to Robert Bridges (1935) Vol. I, pp. 267-8.

15

it generates. Its predominant qualities are energy and exuberance. The job, of eulogy, detraction, or occasional compliment, may appear well done, but the poet's talent has not been modestly subordinated to the one end of his chosen task; on the contrary, it overflows. His best effects suggest that he has only deployed a part of his available resources; he drives faultlessly and courteously and very fast with one hand on the wheel. This is apparent in the ease with which absurdity is given a certain poetic grandeur and even beauty in his humorous passages:

> Besides, his goodly fabric fills the eye,
> And seems design'd for thoughtless majesty;
> Thoughtless as monarch oaks that shade the plain,
> And, spread in solemn state, supinely reign.

This seems to endow Shadwell with a Falstaffian magnificence.

> Then, Israel's monarch, after heaven's own heart,
> His vigorous warmth did variously impart
> To wives and slaves: and, wide as his command,
> Scatter'd his maker's image through the land . . .
> Whether, inspir'd by some diviner lust,
> His father got him with a greater gust . . .

The tone towards Charles II is obviously not that of a poet who is restricting the natural play of his imagination so as to force it into the mould of a political tract for the King's party. Charles's amours and his bastards are delightfully mocked in terms of the Biblical allegory; Dryden has time and skill to demolish Shaftesbury, the King's enemy, in the course of the poem in order to achieve his party end, and at the same time to capture every opportunity of drama and irony that the situation gives him provided only that the main action can still be defined concisely and with propriety.

The faculty of being the spokesman of a group, even of a party, and of yet maintaining artistic integrity is demonstrated again in Dryden's contribution to the Second Part of *Absalom and Achitophel* which was published late in 1682 towards the end of the Exclusion crisis. Only two hundred lines of this part are certainly by Dryden; he seems to have planned the whole poem in broad scenes and descriptions of the Whig party leaders as in Part One, and then handed this programme on to another writer, Nahum Tate, for execution. The fact that his own lines stand out as far more brilliant and interesting than those of Tate should not prevent our marvelling at the way in which Dryden's unassuming workmanship has fitted them in at all. His partisanship is not that of a mere Tory hack; it is based on a commonsense political philosophy contemptuous of certain aspects of Whig theory and faction: one might say it was the political equivalent of Augustan poetic good sense. But above all in this Second Part we remember the splendid energy of exaggeration with which he returns to the attack on the unfortunate Shadwell:

> The midwife laid her hand on his thick skull,
> With this prophetic blessing—*Be thou dull!*
> Drink, swear and roar, forbear no lewd delight
> Fit for thy bulk, do any thing but write.

The sense of great power controlled is present also in the elaborate, irregular choral odes (what in Dryden's time were styled Pindarics). In them he was imitating the effects of different musical instruments:

> Sharp violins proclaim
> Jealous pangs and desperation,
> Fury, frantic indignation,
> For the fair, disdainful dame.

He is thus providing specimens of what can be done by music; the virtuosity combined with the headlong sweep of the long Pindaric stanza and the dexterous transitions from one instrument (and therefore from one represented emotion) to another, create the impression that the poet has at his command the total resources of the art of music and is holding them in reserve; in fact the rhapsodic manner of the poems identifies the poet with

17

Timotheus, the supreme bard, in *Alexander's Feast*, and in the earlier St Cecilia's Day ode, which appears in these selections, with the angel that inspires Cecilia, the genius of music.

The sense of a fluid, natural outburst, splendidly controlled so that it takes the form of art without losing any of its passion, is admirably conveyed by the first stanza of the funeral ode *To Mrs Anne Killigrew*. It is rare to find such a natural tone of voice behind the stiff brocaded splendours of the formal ode. The stanza is a single sentence; it avoids artfulness and affords a firm basis of ordinary pathos from which to take off in a daring Pindaric flight which will identify Anne Killigrew who was unworldly and died young with the unworldly quality at the root of the arts.

> Thou youngest virgin-daughter of the skies,
> Made in the last promotion of the best;
> Whose palms, new pluck'd from paradise,
> In spreading branches more sublimely rise,
> Rich with immortal green above the rest:
> Whether, adopted to some neighbouring star
> Thou roll'st above us, in thy wand'ring race,
>   Or, in procession fix'd and regular,
>   Mov'd with the heavens' majestic pace;
>   Or, call'd to more superior bliss,
> Thou tread'st, with seraphims, the vast abyss:
> Whatever happy region is thy place,
> Cease thy celestial song a little space;
> (Thou wilt have time enough for hymns divine,
>   Since heav'n's eternal year is thine.)
> Hear then a mortal Muse thy praise rehearse,
>   In no ignoble verse;
> But such as thy own voice did practise here,
> When thy first fruits of poesy were giv'n,
> To make thyself a welcome inmate there;
>   While yet a young probationer,
>   And candidate of heav'n.

At another pole of his work his natural vigour redeems the sometimes laboured suggestiveness of the epilogues to his plays.

The Restoration epilogue, spoken after the play by some young actress like Nell Gwynn or Mrs Bracegirdle, worked to a fairly narrow convention of sexual innuendo; in a few stock jokes the gallants in the audience were baited on the score of their morals and their virility. Dryden catches the very essence of the situation in the theatre, its mixture of genuine raffishness and artifice, and writes epilogues that are racy without sniggering. A string of topical obscenities and commonplaces is polished by art and stamped with the earthy robustness of the music-hall.

This vigour and plentifulness (the quality Dryden admired in Chaucer) is not found in Pope, to whom Dryden is so often compared; and Pope is probably more read today. His satirical wit is more finished than anything in Dryden; he concentrates on certain precise ends and brings them to full perfection, where Dryden's grand carelessness leaves loose ends and differing levels of style. Johnson has said the last word on the relation of the two poets to each other in the masterly comparative analysis with which he concludes his *Life of Pope*. Pope is the more finished artist and the more steadily successful as a poet, but it is Dryden who possesses 'that energy which collects, combines, amplifies and animates'. In these words Johnson is describing what Coleridge a few decades later was to define as the special work of the plastic or creative imagination: its power to transform material, however heterogeneous, into a unity. The 'unpoetic' material, the frequent engagement to the conventions of patronage or the theatre, do not matter; these alloys are dissolved in the glow of personal energy he imparts to nearly every work. It may seem stranger to us, in view of the balanced shrewdness that informs so much of the poetry, that Johnson should add in the *Life of Dryden*: 'He delighted to tread upon the brink of meaning, where light and darkness begin to mingle'. But this is Dryden's undoubted verbal daring seen from the point of view of the main poetic tradition after Pope, when a much more settled uniformity had been arrived at. Johnson's remark could be applied most readily to the Pindarics, for instance to the bold and visionary treatment of the Last Judgment in the final stanza of *A Song for St Cecilia's Day* with its echoes of the *Dies Irae*, but even in the poems of discourse an image is often stretched further and made to sink deeper into the consciousness than the precise, prosaic tendency of the later age would permit. In *Religio Laici* Dryden begins with a simile in which he compares the inadequate guidance afforded by the human reason in religious matters to the doubtful light given to benighted travellers by a moon half-hidden by clouds.

> Dim as the borrowed beams of moon and stars
> To lonely, weary, wandering travellers,
> Is reason to the soul.

What might have provided a neat Augustan comparison, antithetically balanced in a single couplet, is drawn out at a slow, meditative pace, the rhythm halting and starting again, so as to capture the very movement of baulked inquiring thought; the image of the moon goes far beyond an initial debating point, and carries into the heart of the argument a sad suggestiveness of the recurring human journey towards knowledge and its accompanying disappointments.

It is worth noticing too that the greater richness of Dryden extends to a command of metres other than the heroic couplet. He can write lyrics, not only the cumbersome Pindarics, but songs like those in the plays with a true singing quality. He is generous and sympathetic to the singer, deliberately curbing meaning for the sake of the melodic line. Even in his heroic couplets the verse trips and sings in the alexandrine lines where an extra foot draws out the measure in a cadenza-like flourish; these lines and the liberal use of triplet rhymes (both devices which Pope abandoned on principle) give a faint air of lyrical pattern to his didactic and satirical poems in the couplet.

To contemplate Dryden's poetic personality without too much attention to historical considerations enables one to understand why Scott called him glorious, and is a healthy corrective to the view which prefers to look at him solely as the architect of the new strict prosody, the master of the school of reason and good sense. The gloriousness, sometimes found in magnificent burlesque as in *Macflecknoe*, sometimes embodied in character as in the fallen beauty of Absalom-Monmouth or the milk-white simplicity of the Hind as the true Church, recalls the symbolic effects of Spenser. In his capacity for grandeur, his humble respect for Shakespeare and his distrust of some aspects of the neo-classical movement, its mechanical theory and artificial eloquence,[1] he stands above his age. But he is also, of course, the architect of revolution. He tempered the neo-classical movement to English needs and entered into the closest possible relationship with the urban literary public, as his prologues and epilogues reveal. Did he really belong to the brittle society of the court and the coffee-houses? More important than belonging, he had helped to create it; he had cast the mould of its myth, the ideal type of reader who is wit and gentleman rather than scholar. He had sounded its keynote, the duty to be easy and natural.

> Correct with spirit, elegant with ease

as Pope said later, but in his case with a tougher masculinity, the grain of the wood showing under the smoothed surface:

> And this unpolish'd, rugged verse I chose
> As fittest for discourse, and nearest prose.

He had assisted at the scaling down to more modest proportions of the Renaissance conception of the poet as a man aspiring to universal knowledge: he and his reader were to be endowed with all the ordinary polite accomplishments; they were no longer 'hydroptic with a sacred thirst', but anxious to stop short of pedantry.

Dryden played a major part in bringing about this useful but often uninspiring compromise because his historical intelligence and his politician's sense of the art of the second best told him

[1] Cf. *Essays*, ed. W. P. Ker, ii. 257.

21

that the 'giant age before the flood' could not be repeated; an era of retrenchment and consolidation was inevitable:

> 'Tis well an old age is out,
> And time to begin a new.

A main feature of the closer, more workmanlike attention to classical models was the cultivation of the 'kinds', the almost sacred genres of poetry, drama, epic, the ode, the epistle, the satire, and so on. Each of these had its appropriate style and diction. One of Dryden's most important legacies was his contribution, chiefly in the translation of the *Aeneid*, to an English heroic and descriptive style of suitable dignity and refinement. For the poetic kinds were arranged in a hierarchy of value, and the epic or heroic poem was the highest form, the summit of possible achievement in humane culture.

Throughout his career Dryden thought and wrote about heroic poetry without writing a true epic himself, though he made plans for one. He thought of his heroic plays as epics in dramatic form, and the shadow of the great poem hangs over both *Absalom and Achitophel* and *The Hind and the Panther*. By Pope's time the great poem is present only as an ironic shadow in the mock epic or mock heroic, a development of the form which Dryden had pioneered in the episode of *Macflecknoe*; the gap between the classical ideal and the London of the Augustans can only be bridged by satiric irony. It is not the least of Dryden's merits that his longer poems, which are well represented in these selections by the whole of *Macflecknoe* and *Absalom and Achitophel*, Part One, and extracts from *The Medal, Annus Mirabilis,* and *The Hind and the Panther*, retain something of the largeness and sweep of true epic. The restraint of literary reform did not prevent him from comprehending and controlling a wide range of ordinary life; after him Pope and the Tory wits turned from it in apocalyptic disgust and left the field to the newly emerging novelists; Dryden is the last poet to celebrate the surface of what Johnson called 'sublunary nature' in the old objective way.

SUGGESTIONS FOR FURTHER READING

WORKS

Poems, edited by James Kinsley (4 vols., Oxford, 1958).

Poems and Fables, edited by James Kinsley (Oxford Standard Authors, 1963). The text of the first work cited without the critical apparatus and notes.

Poetical Works, edited by George R. Noyes (2nd edition, Cambridge, Mass., 1950).

Essays, edited by W. P. Ker (2 vols., Oxford, 1900), or by George Watson (2 vols., Everyman's Library, London, 1962).

Selected Works, edited by William Frost (Rinehart Editions, New York, 1953).

BIOGRAPHY AND CRITICISM

Samuel Johnson, 'Life of Dryden' in *Lives of the Poets*, edited by G. Birkbeck Hill (Oxford, 1905).

Sir Walter Scott, 'Life' in *Works of John Dryden*, edited by Scott and Saintsbury (London, 1882–93).

A. W. Verrall, *Lectures on Dryden* (Cambridge, 1914).

Mark Van Doren, *John Dryden* (London, new edition, 1946).

T. S. Eliot, *John Dryden : the Poet, the Dramatist, the Critic* (London, 1932).

Louis I. Bredvold, *The Intellectual Milieu of John Dryden* (Ann Arbor, 1934).

Ian Jack, *Augustan Satire*, 1660–1740 (Oxford, 1953).

F. T. Prince, 'Dryden Redivivus' in *Review of English Literature*, I (1960).

Charles E. Ward, *The Life of John Dryden* (London, 1961).

William Frost, *Dryden and the Art of Translation* (Berkeley, 1964).

Roger Sharrock, 'Modes of Satire' in *Restoration Theatre*, edited by Bernard Harris (London, 1965).

SELECTED POEMS

To My Honour'd Friend, Dr Charleton

THE longest tyranny that ever sway'd
Was that wherein our ancestors betray'd
Their free-born reason to the Stagirite,
And made his torch their universal light.
So truth, while only one supplied the state,   5
Grew scarce, and dear, and yet sophisticate;
Until 't was bought, like emp'ric wares, or charms,
Hard words seal'd up with Aristotle's arms.
Columbus was the first that shook his throne,
And found a temp'rate in a torrid zone: 10
The fev'rish air fann'd by a cooling breeze,
The fruitful vales set round with shady trees;
And guiltless men, who danc'd away their time,
Fresh as their groves, and happy as their clime.
Had we still paid that homage to a name,   15
Which only God and nature justly claim,
The western seas had been our utmost bound,
Where poets still might dream the sun was drown'd:
And all the stars that shine in southern skies
Had been admir'd by none but salvage eyes.   20
Among th' asserters of free reason's claim,
Th' English are not the least in worth or fame.
The world to Bacon does not only owe
Its present knowledge, but its future too.
Gilbert shall live, till loadstones cease to draw,   25
Or British fleets the boundless ocean awe;

And noble Boyle, not less in nature seen,
Than his great brother read in states and men.
The circling streams, once thought but pools, of blood
(Whether life's fuel, or the body's food)   30
From dark oblivion Harvey's name shall save;
While Ent keeps all the honour that he gave.
Nor are *you*, learned friend, the least renown'd;
Whose fame, not circumscrib'd with English ground,
Flies like the nimble journeys of the light;   35
And is, like that, unspent too in its flight.
Whatever truths have been, by art or chance,
Redeem'd from error, or from ignorance,
Thin in their authors, like rich veins of ore,
Your works unite, and still discover more.   40
Such is the healing virtue of your pen,
To perfect cures on books, as well as men.
Nor is this work the least: you well may give
To men new vigour, who make stones to live.
Thro' you, the Danes, their short dominion lost,   45
A longer conquest than the Saxons boast.
Stonehenge, once thought a temple, you have found
A throne, where kings, our earthly gods, were crown'd;
Where by their wond'ring subjects they were seen,
Joy'd with their stature, and their princely mien.   50
Our sovereign here above the rest might stand,
And here be chose again to rule the land.
These ruins shelter'd once his sacred head,
Then when from Wor'ster's fatal field he fled;
Watch'd by the genius of this royal place,   55
And mighty visions of the Danish race.
His refuge then was for a temple shown;
But, he restor'd, 't is now become a throne.

Annus Mirabilis

CCXCIII

Methinks already, from this chymic flame,
   I see a city of more precious mould,   1170
Rich as the town which gives the Indies name,
   With silver pav'd, and all divine with gold.

CCXCIV

Already, labouring with a mighty fate,
   She shakes the rubbish from her mounting brow,
And seems to have renew'd her charter's date,   1175
   Which Heav'n will to the death of time allow.

CCXCV

More great than human, now, and more august.
   New-deified she from her fires does rise:
Her widening streets on new foundations trust,
   And, opening, into larger parts she flies.   1180

CCXCVI

Before, she like some shepherdess did show,
   Who sate to bathe her by a river's side;
Not answering to her fame, but rude and low,
   Nor taught the beauteous arts of modern pride.

CCXCVII

Now, like a maiden queen, she will behold,   1185
   From her high turrets, hourly suitors come:
The East with incense, and the West with gold,
   Will stand, like suppliants, to receive her doom.

CCXCVIII

The silver Thames, her own domestic flood,
 Shall bear her vessels like a sweeping train; 1190
And often wind, (as of his mistress proud,)
 With longing eyes to meet her face again.

CCXCIX

The wealthy Tagus, and the wealthier Rhine,
 The glory of their towns no more shall boast;
And Seine, that would with Belgian rivers join, 1195
 Shall find her lustre stain'd, and traffic lost.

CCC

The vent'rous merchant, who design'd more far,
 And touches on our hospitable shore,
Charm'd with the splendour of this northern star,
 Shall here unlade him, and depart no more. 1200

CCCI

Our pow'rful navy shall no longer meet,
 The wealth of France or Holland to invade;
The beauty of this town, without a fleet,
 From all the world shall vindicate her trade.

CCCII

And, while this fam'd emporium we prepare, 1205
 The British ocean shall such triumphs boast,
That those who now disdain our trade to share,
 Shall rob like pirates on our wealthy coast.

CCCIII

Already we have conquer'd half the war,
 And the less dang'rous part is left behind; 1210
Our trouble now is but to make them dare,
 And not so great to vanquish as to find.

Thus to the eastern wealth thro' storms we go,
  But now, the Cape once doubled, fear no more;
A constant trade-wind will securely blow,   1215
  And gently lay us on the spicy shore.

Epilogue to Tyrannick Love

SPOKEN BY MRS ELLEN, WHEN SHE WAS TO
BE CARRIED OFF DEAD BY THE BEARERS

[*To the Bearer.*]   Hold, are you mad? you damn'd
    confounded dog,
I am to rise, and speak the epilogue.
  [*To the Audience.*]   I come, kind gentlemen, strange
    news to tell ye,
I am the ghost of poor departed Nelly.
Sweet ladies, be not frighted, I 'll be civil;   5
I 'm what I was, a little harmless devil:
For after death, we sprites have just such natures
We had for all the world, when human creatures;
And therefore I that was an actress here,
Play all my tricks in hell, a goblin there.   10
Gallants, look to 't, you say there are no sprites;
But I 'll come dance about your beds at nights.
And faith you'll be in a sweet kind of taking,
When I surprise you between sleep and waking.
To tell you true, I walk because I die   15
Out of my calling in a tragedy.
O poet, damn'd dull poet, who could prove
So senseless! to make Nelly die for love!
Nay, what 's yet worse, to kill me in the prime
Of Easter term, in tart and cheese-cake time!   20

I 'll fit the fop, for I 'll not one word say
T' excuse his godly out-of-fashion play:
A play, which if you dare but twice sit out,
You 'll all be slander'd, and be thought devout.
But farewell, gentlemen, make haste to me;   25
I 'm sure ere long to have your company.
As for my epitaph, when I am gone,
I 'll trust no poet, but will write my own:

Here Nelly lies, who, tho' she liv'd a slattern,
Yet died a princess, acting in St Cathar'n.   30

Epilogue to the Second Part of *The Conquest of Granada*

THEY who have best succeeded on the stage:
Have still conform'd their genius to their age.
Thus Jonson did mechanic humour show,
When men were dull, and conversation low.
Then comedy was faultless, but 't was coarse: 5
Cob's tankard was a jest, and Otter's horse.
And, as their comedy, their love was mean;
Except, by chance, in some one labour'd scene
Which must atone for an ill-written play.
They rose, but at their height could seldom stay.   10
Fame then was cheap, and the first comer sped;
And they have kept it since, by being dead.
But, were they now to write, when critics weigh
Each line, and ev'ry word, throughout a play,
None of 'em, no, not Jonson in his height,   15
Could pass, without allowing grains for weight.

Think it not envy, that these truths are told;
Our poet 's not malicious, tho' he 's bold.
'T is not to brand 'em, that their faults are shown,
But, by their errors, to excuse his own.   20
If love and honour now are higher rais'd.
'T is not the poet, but the age is prais'd.
Wit 's now arriv'd to a more high degree;
Our native language more refin'd and free.
Our ladies and our men now speak more wit   25
In conversation, than those poets writ.
Then, one of these is, consequently, true;
That what this poet writes comes short of you,
And imitates you ill, (which most he fears,)
Or else his writing is not worse than theirs.   30
Yet, tho' you judge (as sure the critics will)
That some before him writ with greater skill,
In this one praise he has their fame surpass'd,
To please an age more gallant than the last.

Song from Marriage à la Mode

I

WHY should a foolish marriage vow,
    Which long ago was made,
Oblige us to each other now,
    When passion is decay'd?
We lov'd, and we lov'd, as long as we could,   5
    Till our love was lov'd out in us both;
But our marriage is dead, when the pleasure is fled:
    'T was pleasure first made it an oath.

33

If I have pleasures for a friend,
  And farther love in store,   10
What wrong has he whose joys did end,
  And who could give no more?
'T is a madness that he should be jealous of me,
  Or that I should bar him of another:
For all we can gain is to give ourselves pain,   15
  When neither can hinder the other.

Prologue to the University of Oxford, 1674

SPOKEN BY MR HART

POETS, your subjects, have their parts assign'd
T' unbend, and to divert their sovereign's mind:
When tir'd with following nature, you think fit
To seek repose in the cool shades of wit,
And, from the sweet retreat, with joy survey   5
What rests, and what is conquer'd, of the way.
Here, free yourselves from envy, care, and strife,
You view the various turns of human life:
Safe in our scene, thro' dangerous courts you go,
And, undebauch'd, the vice of cities know.   10
Your theories are here to practice brought,
As in mechanic operations wrought;
And man, the little world, before you set,
As once the sphere of crystal shew'd the great.
Blest sure are you above all mortal kind,   15
If to your fortunes you can suit your mind:

Content to see, and shun, those ills we show,
And crimes on theatres alone to know,
With joy we bring what our dead authors writ,
And beg from you the value of their wit: 20
That Shakespeare's, Fletcher's, and great Jonson's claim
May be renew'd from those who gave them fame.
None of your living poets dare appear;
For Muses so severe are worshipp'd here,
That, conscious of their faults, they shun the eye, 25
And, as profane, from sacred places fly,
Rather than see th' offended God, and die.
We bring no imperfections but our own;
Such faults as made are by the makers shown:
And you have been so kind, that we may boast, 30
The greatest judges still can pardon most.
Poets must stoop, when they would please our pit,
Debas'd even to the level of their wit;
Disdaining that which yet they know will take,
Hating themselves what their applause must make. 35
But when to praise from you they would aspire,
Tho' they like eagles mount, your Jove is higher.
So far your knowledge all their pow'r transcends
As what *should* be, beyond what *is,* extends.

Prologue to Aureng-Zebe

OUR author, by experience, finds it true,
'T is much more hard to please himself than you;
And out of no feign'd modesty, this day
Damns his laborious trifle of a play:
Not that it 's worse than what before he writ, 5

But he has now another taste of wit;
And, to confess a truth, (tho' out of time,)
Grows weary of his long-lov'd mistress, Rhyme.
Passion 's too fierce to be in fetters bound,
And nature flies him like enchanted ground.   10
What verse can do, he has perform'd in this,
Which he presumes the most correct of his;
But spite of all his pride, a secret shame
Invades his breast at Shakespeare's sacred name:
Aw'd when he heard his godlike Romans rage,   15
He, in a just despair, would quit the stage;
And to an age less polish'd, more unskill'd,
Does, with disdain, the foremost honours yield.
As with the greater dead he dares not strive,
He would not match his verse with those who live: 20
Let him retire, betwixt two ages cast,
The first of this, and hindmost of the last.
A losing gamester, let him sneak away;
He bears no ready money from the play.
The fate which governs poets thought it fit   25
He should not raise his fortunes by his wit.
The clergy thrive, and the litigious bar;
Dull heroes fatten with the spoils of war:
All southern vices, Heav'n be prais'd, are here;
But wit 's a luxury you think too dear.   30
When you to cultivate the plant are loth,
'T is a shrewd sign 't was never of your growth;
And wit in northern climates will not blow,
Except, like orange trees, 't is hous'd from snow.
There needs no care to put a playhouse down,   35
'T is the most desart place of all the town:
We and our neighbours, to speak proudly, are,
Like monarchs, ruin'd with expensive war;
While, like wise English, unconcern'd you sit,
And see us play the tragedy of wit.   40

Song from *The Spanish Friar*

I

FAREWELL, ungrateful traitor!
    Farewell, my perjur'd swain!
Let never injur'd creature
    Believe a man again.
The pleasure of possessing   5
Surpasses all expressing,
But 't is too short a blessing,
    And love too long a pain.

II

'T is easy to deceive us,
    In pity of your pain;   10
But when we love, you leave us
    To rail at you in vain.
Before we have descried it,
There is no bliss beside it;
But she that once has tried it,   15
    Will never love again.

III

The passion you pretended,
    Was only to obtain;
But when the charm is ended,
    The charmer you disdain.   20
Your love by ours we measure,
Till we have lost our treasure;
But dying is a pleasure,
    When living is a pain.

37

Absalom and Achitophel

PART ONE

In pious times, ere priestcraft did begin,
Before polygamy was made a sin;
When man on many multiplied his kind,
Ere one to one was cursedly confin'd;
When nature prompted, and no law denied   5
Promiscuous use of concubine and bride;
Then Israel's monarch after Heaven's own heart,
His vigorous warmth did variously impart
To wives and slaves; and, wide as his command,
Scatter'd his Maker's image thro' the land.   10
Michal, of royal blood, the crown did wear;
A soil ungrateful to the tiller's care:
Not so the rest; for several mothers bore
To godlike David several sons before.
But since like slaves his bed they did ascend,   15
No true succession could their seed attend.
Of all this numerous progeny was none
So beautiful, so brave, as Absalon:
Whether, inspir'd by some diviner lust,
His father got him with a greater gust;   20
Or that his conscious destiny made way,
By manly beauty, to imperial sway.
Early in foreign fields he won renown,
With kings and states allied to Israel's crown
In peace the thoughts of war he could remove,   25
And seem'd as he were only born for love.
Whate'er he did, was done with so much ease,

In him alone 't was natural to please:
His motions all accompanied with grace;
And paradise was open'd in his face. 30
With secret joy indulgent David view'd
His youthful image in his son renew'd:
To all his wishes nothing he denied;
And made the charming Annabel his bride.
What faults he had, (for who from faults is free?) 35
His father could not, or he would not see.
Some warm excesses which the law forbore,
Were construed youth that purg'd by boiling o'er,
And Amnon's murther, by a specious name,
Was call'd a just revenge for injur'd fame. 40
Thus prais'd and lov'd the noble youth remain'd,
While David, undisturb'd, in Sion reign'd.
But life can never be sincerely blest;
Heav'n punishes the bad, and proves the best.
The Jews, a headstrong, moody, murm'ring race, 45
As ever tried th' extent and stretch of grace;
God's pamper'd people, whom, debauch'd with ease,
No king could govern, nor no God could please;
(Gods they had tried of every shape and size,
That god-smiths could produce, or priests devise:) 50
These Adam-wits, too fortunately free,
Began to dream they wanted liberty;
And when no rule, no precedent was found,
Of men by laws less circumscrib'd and bound;
They led their wild desires to woods and caves, 55
And thought that all but savages were slaves.
They who, when Saul was dead, without a blow,
Made foolish Ishbosheth the crown forego;
Who banish'd David did from Hebron bring,
And with a general shout proclaim'd him king: 60
Those very Jews, who, at their very best,
Their humour more than loyalty express'd,

Now wonder'd why so long they had obey'd
An idol monarch, which their hands had made;
Thought they might ruin him they could create,   65
Or melt him to that golden calf, a State.
But these were random bolts; no form'd design,
Nor interest made the factious crowd to join:
The sober part of Israel, free from stain,
Well knew the value of a peaceful reign;   70
And, looking backward with a wise affright,
Saw seams of wounds, dishonest to the sight:
In contemplation of whose ugly scars
They curs'd the memory of civil wars.
The moderate sort of men, thus qualified,   75
Inclin'd the balance to the better side;
And David's mildness manag'd it so well,
The bad found no occasion to rebel.
But when to sin our bias'd nature leans,
The careful Devil is still at hand with means;   80
And providently pimps for ill desires.
The Good Old Cause reviv'd, a plot requires:
Plots, true or false, are necessary things,
To raise up commonwealths, and ruin kings.
    Th' inhabitants of old Jerusalem   85
Were Jebusites; the town so call'd from them;
And theirs the native right ——
But when the chosen people grew more strong,
The rightful cause at length became the wrong;
And every loss the men of Jebus bore,   90
They still were thought God's enemies the more.
Thus worn and weaken'd, well or ill content,
Submit they must to David's government:
Impoverish'd and depriv'd of all command,
Their taxes doubled as they lost their land;   95
And, what was harder yet to flesh and blood,
Their gods disgrac'd, and burnt like common wood.

This set the heathen priesthood in a flame;
For priests of all religions are the same:
Of whatsoe'er descent their godhead be, 100
Stock, stone, or other homely pedigree,
In his defence his servants are as bold,
As if he had been born of beaten gold.
The Jewish rabbins, tho' their enemies,
In this conclude them honest men and wise: 105
For 't was their duty, all the learned think,
T' espouse his cause, by whom they eat and drink.
From hence began that Plot, the nation's curse,
Bad in itself, but represented worse;
Rais'd in extremes, and in extremes decried; 110
With oaths affirm'd, with dying vows denied;
Not weigh'd or winnow'd by the multitude;
But swallow'd in the mass, unchew'd and crude.
Some truth there was, but dash'd and brew'd with lies,
To please the fools, and puzzle all the wise. 115
Succeeding times did equal folly call,
Believing nothing, or believing all.
Th' Egyptian rites the Jebusites embrac'd;
Where gods were recommended by their taste.
Such sav'ry deities must needs be good, 120
As serv'd at once for worship and for food.
By force they could not introduce these gods,
For ten to one in former days was odds;
So fraud was us'd (the sacrificer's trade):
Fools are more hard to conquer than persuade. 125
Their busy teachers mingled with the Jews,
And rak'd for converts even the court and stews:
Which Hebrew priests the more unkindly took,
Because the fleece accompanies the flock.
Some thought they God's anointed meant to slay 130
By guns, invented since full many a day:
Our author swears it not; but who can know

41

How far the Devil and Jebusites may go?
This Plot, which fail'd for want of common sense,
Had yet a deep and dangerous consequence: 135
For, as when raging fevers boil the blood,
The standing lake soon floats into a flood,
And ev'ry hostile humour, which before
Slept quiet in its channels, bubbles o'er;
So several factions from this first ferment   140
Work up to foam, and threat the government.
Some by their friends, more by themselves thought wise,
Oppos'd the pow'r to which they could not rise.
Some had in courts been great, and thrown from thence,
Like fiends were harden'd in impenitence.   145
Some, by their monarch's fatal mercy, grown
From pardon'd rebels kinsmen to the throne,
Were rais'd in pow'r and public office high;
Strong bands, if bands ungrateful men could tie.
    Of these the false Achitophel was first;   150
A name to all succeeding ages curst:
For close designs and crooked counsels fit;
Sagacious, bold, and turbulent of wit;
Restless, unfix'd in principles and place;
In pow'r unpleas'd, impatient of disgrace: 155
A fiery soul, which, working out its way,
Fretted the pigmy body to decay,
And o'er-inform'd the tenement of clay.
A daring pilot in extremity;
Pleas'd with the danger, when the waves went high,   160
He sought the storms; but, for a calm unfit,
Would steer too nigh the sands, to boast his wit.
Great wits are sure to madness near allied,
And thin partitions do their bounds divide;
Else why should he, with wealth and honour blest,   165
Refuse his age the needful hours of rest?
Punish a body which he could not please;

42

Bankrupt of life, yet prodigal of ease?
And all to leave what with his toil he won,
To that unfeather'd two-legg'd thing, a son;   170
Got, while his soul did huddled notions try;
And born a shapeless lump, like anarchy.
In friendship false, implacable in hate;
Resolv'd to ruin or to rule the State.
To compass this the triple bond he broke;   175
The pillars of the public safety shook;
And fitted Israel for a foreign yoke:
Then seiz'd with fear, yet still affecting fame,
Usurp'd a patriot's all-atoning name.
So easy still it proves in factious times,   180
With public zeal to cancel private crimes.
How safe is treason, and how sacred ill,
Where none can sin against the people's will!
Where crowds can wink, and no offence be known,
Since in another's guilt they find their own!   185
Yet fame deserv'd no enemy can grudge;
The statesman we abhor, but praise the judge.
In Israel's courts ne'er sat an Abbethdin
With more discerning eyes, or hands more clean;
Unbrib'd, unsought, the wretched to redress;   190
Swift of dispatch, and easy of access.
O, had he been content to serve the crown,
With virtues only proper to the gown;
Or had the rankness of the soil been freed
From cockle, that oppress'd the noble seed;   195
David for him his tuneful harp had strung,
And Heav'n had wanted one immortal song.
But wild Ambition loves to slide, not stand,
And Fortune's ice prefers to Virtue's land.
Achitophel, grown weary to possess   200
A lawful fame, and lazy happiness,
Disdain'd the golden fruit to gather free,

43

And lent the crowd his arm to shake the tree.
Now, manifest of crimes contriv'd long since,
He stood at bold defiance with his prince;　　205
Held up the buckler of the people's cause
Against the crown, and skulk'd behind the laws.
The wish'd occasion of the Plot he takes;
Some circumstances finds, but more he makes.
By buzzing emissaries fills the ears　　210
Of list'ning crowds with jealousies and fears
Of arbitrary counsels brought to light,
And proves the king himself a Jebusite.
Weak arguments! which yet he knew full well
Were strong with people easy to rebel.　　215
For, govern'd by the moon, the giddy Jews
Tread the same track when she the prime renews;
And once in twenty years, their scribes record,
By natural instinct they change their lord.
Achitophel still wants a chief, and none　　220
Was found so fit as warlike Absalon:
Not that he wish'd his greatness to create,
(For politicians neither love nor hate,)
But, for he knew his title not allow'd,
Would keep him still depending on the crowd:　　225
That kingly pow'r, thus ebbing out, might be
Drawn to the dregs of a democracy.
Him he attempts with studied arts to please,
And sheds his venom in such words as these:

"Auspicious prince, at whose nativity　　230
Some royal planet rul'd the southern sky;
Thy longing country's darling and desire;
Their cloudy pillar and their guardian fire:
Their second Moses, whose extended wand
Divides the seas, and shews the promis'd land;　　235
Whose dawning day in every distant age
Has exercis'd the sacred prophets' rage:

44

The people's pray'r, the glad diviners' theme,
The young men's vision, and the old men's dream!
Thee, Saviour, thee, the nation's vows confess,   240
And, never satisfied with seeing, bless:
Swift unbespoken pomps thy steps proclaim,
And stammering babes are taught to lisp thy name.
How long wilt thou the general joy detain,
Starve and defraud the people of thy reign?   245
Content ingloriously to pass thy days
Like one of Virtue's fools that feeds on praise;
Till thy fresh glories, which now shine so bright,
Grow stale and tarnish with our daily sight.
Believe me, royal youth, thy fruit must be   250
Or gather'd ripe, or rot upon the tree.
Heav'n has to all allotted, soon or late,
Some lucky revolution of their fate;
Whose motions if we watch and guide with skill,
(For human good depends on human will,)   255
Our Fortune rolls as from a smooth descent,
And from the first impression takes the bent:
But, if unseiz'd, she glides away like wind,
And leaves repenting Folly far behind.
Now, now she meets you with a glorious prize,   260
And spreads her locks before her as she flies.
Had thus old David, from whose loins you spring,
Not dar'd, when Fortune call'd him, to be king,
At Gath an exile he might still remain,
And Heaven's anointing oil had been in vain.   265
Let his successful youth your hopes engage;
But shun th' example of declining age:
Behold him setting in his western skies,
The shadows lengthening as the vapours rise
He is not now, as when on Jordan's sand   270
The joyful people throng'd to see him land,
Cov'ring the beach, and black'ning all the strand;

But, like the Prince of Angels, from his height
Comes tumbling downward with diminish'd light;
Betray'd by one poor plot to public scorn,   275
(Our only blessing since his curst return;)
Those heaps of people which one sheaf did bind,
Blown off and scatter'd by a puff of wind.
What strength can he to your designs oppose,
Naked of friends, and round beset with foes?   280
If Pharaoh's doubtful succour he should use,
A foreign aid would more incense the Jews:
Proud Egypt would dissembled friendship bring;
Foment the war, but not support the king:
Nor would the royal party e'er unite   285
With Pharaoh's arms t' assist the Jebusite;
Or if they should, their interest soon would break,
And with such odious aid make David weak.
All sorts of men by my successful arts,
Abhorring kings, estrange their alter'd hearts   290
From David's rule: and 't is the general cry,
'Religion, commonwealth, and liberty.'
If you, as champion of the public good,
Add to their arms a chief of royal blood,
What may not Israel hope, and what applause   295
Might such a general gain by such a cause?
Not barren praise alone, that gaudy flow'r
Fair only to the sight, but solid pow'r;
And nobler is a limited command,
Giv'n by the love of all your native land,   300
Than a successive title, long and dark,
Drawn from the mouldy rolls of Noah's ark."
    What cannot praise effect in mighty minds,
When flattery soothes, and when ambition blinds!
Desire of pow'r, on earth a vicious weed,   305
Yet, sprung from high, is of celestial seed:
In God 't is glory; and when men aspire,

46

'T is but a spark too much of heavenly fire.
Th' ambitious youth, too covetous of fame,
Too full of angels' metal in his frame,   310
Unwarily was led from virtue's ways,
Made drunk with honour, and debauch'd with praise.
Half loth, and half consenting to the ill,
(For loyal blood within him struggled still,)
He thus replied: "And what pretence have I   315
To take up arms for public liberty?
My father governs with unquestion'd right;
The faith's defender, and mankind's delight;
Good, gracious, just, observant of the laws:
And Heav'n by wonders has espous'd his cause.   320
Whom has he wrong'd in all his peaceful reign?
Who sues for justice to his throne in vain?
What millions has he pardon'd of his foes,
Whom just revenge did to his wrath expose?
Mild, easy, humble, studious of our good;   325
Enclin'd to mercy, and averse from blood;
If mildness ill with stubborn Israel suit,
His crime is God's beloved attribute.
What could he gain, his people to betray,
Or change his right for arbitrary sway?   330
Let haughty Pharaoh curse with such a reign
His fruitful Nile, and yoke a servile train.
If David's rule Jerusalem displease,
The Dog-star heats their brains to this disease.
Why then should I, encouraging the bad,   335
Turn rebel and run popularly mad?
Were he a tyrant, who, by lawless might
Oppress'd the Jews, and rais'd the Jebusite,
Well might I mourn; but nature's holy bands
Would curb my spirits and restrain my hands: 340
The people might assert their liberty;
But what was right in them were crime in me.

47

His favour leaves me nothing to require,
Prevents my wishes, and outruns desire.
What more can I expect while David lives?   345
All but his kingly diadem he gives:
And that" — But there he paus'd; then sighing, said —
"Is justly destin'd for a worthier head.
For when my father from his toils shall rest,
And late augment the number of the blest,   350
His lawful issue shall the throne ascend,
Or the *collat'ral* line, where that shall end.
His brother, tho' oppress'd with vulgar spite,
Yet dauntless, and secure of native right,
Of every royal virtue stands possess'd;   355
Still dear to all the bravest and the best.
His courage foes, his friends his truth proclaim;
His loyalty the king, the world his fame.
His mercy ev'n th' offending crowd will find;
For sure he comes of a forgiving kind.   360
Why should I then repine at Heaven's decree,
Which gives me no pretence to royalty?
Yet O that fate, propitiously inclin'd,
Had rais'd my birth, or had debas'd my mind;
To my large soul not all her treasure lent,   365
And then betray'd it to a mean descent!
I find, I find my mounting spirits bold,
And David's part disdains my mother's mould.
Why am I scanted by a niggard birth?
My soul disclaims the kindred of her earth;   370
And, made for empire, whispers me within,
'Desire of greatness is a godlike sin.' "
   Him staggering so when hell's dire agent found,
While fainting Virtue scarce maintain'd her ground,
He pours fresh forces in, and thus replies: 375
   "Th' eternal God, supremely good and wise,
Imparts not these prodigious gifts in vain:

48

What wonders are reserv'd to bless your reign!
Against your will, your arguments have shown,
Such virtue's only giv'n to guide a throne.   380
Not that your father's mildness I contemn;
But manly force becomes the diadem.
'T is true he grants the people all they crave;
And more, perhaps, than subjects ought to have:
For lavish grants suppose a monarch tame,   385
And more his goodness than his wit proclaim.
But when should people strive their bonds to break,
If not when kings are negligent or weak?
Let him give on till he can give no more,
The thrifty Sanhedrin shall keep him poor;   390
And every shekel which he can receive,
Shall cost a limb of his prerogative.
To ply him with new plots shall be my care;
Or plunge him deep in some expensive war;
Which when his treasure can no more supply,   395
He must, with the remains of kingship, buy.
His faithful friends, our jealousies and fears
Call Jebusites, and Pharaoh's pensioners;
Whom when our fury from his aid has torn,
He shall be naked left to public scorn.   400
The next successor, whom I fear and hate,
My arts have made obnoxious to the State;
Turn'd all his virtues to his overthrow,
And gain'd our elders to pronounce a foe.
His right, for sums of necessary gold,   405
Shall first be pawn'd, and afterwards be sold;
Till time shall ever-wanting David draw,
To pass your doubtful title into law:
If not, the people have a right supreme
To make their kings; for kings are made for them.   410
All empire is no more than pow'r in trust,
Which, when resum'd, can be no longer just.

Succession, for the general good design'd
In its own wrong a nation cannot bind;
If altering that the people can relieve,   415
Better one suffer than a nation grieve.
The Jews well know their pow'r: ere Saul they chose,
God was their king, and God they durst depose.
Urge now your piety, your filial name,
A father's right, and fear of future fame;   420
The public good, that universal call,
To which even Heav'n submitted, answers all.
Nor let his love enchant your generous mind;
'T is Nature's trick to propagate her kind.
Our fond begetters, who would never die,   425
Love but themselves in their posterity.
Or let his kindness by th' effects be tried,
Or let him lay his vain pretence aside.
God said he lov'd your father; could he bring
A better proof, than to anoint him king?   430
It surely shew'd he lov'd the shepherd well,
Who gave so fair a flock as Israel.
Would David have you thought his darling son?
What means he then, to alienate the crown?
The name of godly he may blush to bear: 435
'T is after God's own heart to cheat his heir.
He to his brother gives supreme command,
To you a legacy of barren land:
Perhaps th' old harp, on which he thrums his lays,
Or some dull Hebrew ballad in your praise.   440
Then the next heir, a prince severe and wise,
Already looks on you with jealous eyes;
Sees thro' the thin disguises of your arts,
And marks your progress in the people's hearts.
Tho' now his mighty soul its grief contains,   445
He meditates revenge who least complains;
And, like a lion, slumb'ring in the way,

50

Or sleep dissembling, while he waits his prey,
His fearless foes within his distance draws,
Constrains his roaring, and contracts his paws;   450
Till at the last, his time for fury found,
He shoots with sudden vengeance from the ground;
The prostrate vulgar passes o'er and spares,
But with a lordly rage his hunters tears.
Your case no tame expedients will afford: 455
Resolve on death, or conquest by the sword,
Which for no less a stake than life you draw;
And self-defence is nature's eldest law.
Leave the warm people no considering time;
For then rebellion may be thought a crime.   460
Prevail yourself of what occasion gives,
But try your title while your father lives;
And that your arms may have a fair pretence,
Proclaim you take them in the king's defence;
Whose sacred life each minute would expose   465
To plots, from seeming friends, and secret foes.
And who can sound the depth of David's soul?
Perhaps his fear his kindness may control.
He fears his brother, tho' he loves his son,
For plighted vows too late to be undone.   470
If so, by force he wishes to be gain'd;
Like women's lechery, to seem constrain'd.
Doubt not: but, when he most affects the frown,
Commit a pleasing rape upon the crown.
Secure his person to secure your cause: 475
They who possess the prince, possess the laws."

    He said, and this advice above the rest,
With Absalom's mild nature suited best:
Unblam'd of life, (ambition set aside,)
Not stain'd with cruelty, nor puff'd with pride;   480
How happy had he been, if destiny
Had higher plac'd his birth, or not so high!

His kingly virtues might have claim'd a throne,
And blest all other countries but his own.
But charming greatness since so few refuse, 485
'T is juster to lament him than accuse.
Strong were his hopes a rival to remove,
With blandishments to gain the public love;
To head the faction while their zeal was hot,
And popularly prosecute the Plot. 490
To farther this, Achitophel unites
The malcontents of all the Israelites;
Whose differing parties he could wisely join,
For several ends, to serve the same design:
The best, (and of the princes some were such,) 495
Who thought the pow'r of monarchy too much;
Mistaken men, and patriots in their hearts;
Not wicked, but seduc'd by impious arts.
By these the springs of property were bent,
And wound so high, they crack'd the government. 500
The next for interest sought t' embroil the State,
To sell their duty at a dearer rate;
And make their Jewish markets of the throne,
Pretending public good, to serve their own.
Others thought kings an useless heavy load, 505
Who cost too much, and did too little good.
These were for laying honest David by,
On principles of pure good husbandry.
With them join'd all th' haranguers of the throng,
That thought to get preferment by the tongue. 510
Who follow next, a double danger bring,
Not only hating David, but the king:
The Solymæan rout, well-vers'd of old
In godly faction, and in treason bold;
Cow'ring and quaking at a conqu'ror's sword; 515
But lofty to a lawful prince restor'd;
Saw with disdain an Ethnic plot begun,

And scorn'd by Jebusites to be outdone.
Hot Levites headed these; who, pull'd before
From th' ark, which in the Judges' days they bore,   520
Resum'd their cant, and with a zealous cry
Pursued their old belov'd Theocracy:
Where Sanhedrin and priest enslav'd the nation,
And justified their spoils by inspiration:
For who so fit for reign as Aaron's race,   525
If once dominion they could found in grace;
These led the pack; tho' not of surest scent,
Yet deepest mouth'd against the government.
A numerous host of dreaming saints succeed,
Of the true old enthusiastic breed: 530
'Gainst form and order they their pow'r imploy,
Nothing to build, and all things to destroy.
But far more numerous was the herd of such,
Who think too little, and who talk too much.
These, out of mere instinct, they knew not why,   535
Ador'd their fathers' God and property;
And, by the same blind benefit of fate,
The Devil and the Jebusite did hate:
Born to be sav'd, even in their own despite,
Because they could not help believing right.   540
Such were the tools; but a whole Hydra more
Remains, of sprouting heads too long to score.
Some of their chiefs were princes of the land:
In the first rank of these did Zimri stand;
A man so various, that he seem'd to be   545
Not one, but all mankind's epitome:
Stiff in opinions, always in the wrong;
Was everything by starts, and nothing long,
But, in the course of one revolving moon,
Was chymist, fiddler, statesman, and buffoon: 550
Then all for women, painting, rhyming, drinking,
Besides ten thousand freaks that died in thinking.

Blest madman, who could every hour employ,
With something new to wish, or to enjoy!
Railing and praising were his usual themes;   555
And both (to shew his judgment) in extremes:
So over-violent, or over-civil,
That every man, with him, was God or Devil.
In squand'ring wealth was his peculiar art:
Nothing went unrewarded but desert.   560
Beggar'd by fools, whom still he found too late,
He had his jest, and they had his estate.
He laugh'd himself from court; then sought relief
By forming parties, but could ne'er be chief;
For, spite of him, the weight of business fell   565
On Absalom and wise Achitophel:
Thus, wicked but in will, of means bereft,
He left not faction, but of that was left.
   Titles and names 't were tedious to rehearse
Of lords, below the dignity of verse.   570
Wits, warriors, Commonwealth's-men, were the best;
Kind husbands, and mere nobles, all the rest.
And therefore, in the name of dulness, be
The well-hung Balaam and cold Caleb, free;
And canting Nadab let oblivion damn,   575
Who made new porridge for the paschal lamb.
Let friendship's holy band some names assure;
Some their own worth, and some let scorn secure.
Nor shall the rascal rabble here have place,
Whom kings no titles gave, and God no grace: 580
Not bull-fac'd Jonas, who could statutes draw
To mean rebellion, and make treason law.
But he, tho' bad, is follow'd by a worse,
The wretch who Heav'n's anointed dar'd to curse:
Shimei, whose youth did early promise bring   585
Of zeal to God and hatred to his king,
Did wisely from expensive sins refrain,

And never broke the Sabbath, but for gain;
Nor ever was he known an oath to vent,
Or curse, unless against the government. 590
Thus heaping wealth, by the most ready way
Among the Jews, which was to cheat and pray,
The city, to reward his pious hate
Against his master, chose him magistrate.
His hand a vare of justice did uphold; 595
His neck was loaded with a chain of gold.
During his office, treason was no crime;
The sons of Belial had a glorious time;
For Shimei, tho' not prodigal of pelf,
Yet lov'd his wicked neighbour as himself. 600
When two or three were gather'd to declaim
Against the monarch of Jerusalem,
Shimei was always in the midst of them;
And if they curs'd the king when he was by,
Would rather curse than break good company. 605
If any durst his factious friends accuse,
He pack'd a jury of dissenting Jews;
Whose fellow-feeling in the godly cause
Would free the suff'ring saint from human laws.
For laws are only made to punish those 610
Who serve the king, and to protect his foes.
If any leisure time he had from pow'r,
(Because 't is sin to misimploy an hour,)
His bus'ness was, by writing, to persuade
That kings were useless, and a clog to trade; 615
And, that his noble style he might refine,
No Rechabite more shunn'd the fumes of wine.
Chaste were his cellars, and his shrieval board
The grossness of a city feast abhorr'd:
His cooks, with long disuse, their trade forgot; 620
Cool was his kitchen, tho' his brains were hot.
Such frugal virtue malice may accuse,

But sure 't was necessary to the Jews;
For towns once burnt such magistrates require
As dare not tempt God's providence by fire.   625
With spiritual food he fed his servants well,
But free from flesh that made the Jews rebel;
And Moses' laws he held in more account,
For forty days of fasting in the mount.

To speak the rest, who better are forgot,   630
Would tire a well-breath'd witness of the Plot.
Yet, Corah, thou shalt from oblivion pass:
Erect thyself, thou monumental brass,
High as the serpent of thy metal made,
While nations stand secure beneath thy shade.   635
What tho' his birth were base, yet comets rise
From earthy vapours, ere they shine in skies.
Prodigious actions may as well be done
By weaver's issue, as by prince's son.
This arch-attestor for the public good   640
By that one deed ennobles all his blood.
Who ever ask'd the witnesses' high race,
Whose oath with martyrdom did Stephen grace?
Ours was a Levite, and as times went then,
His tribe were God Almighty's gentlemen.   645
Sunk were his eyes, his voice was harsh and loud,
Sure signs he neither choleric was nor proud:
His long chin prov'd his wit; his saintlike grace
A church vermilion, and a Moses' face.
His memory, miraculously great,   650
Could plots, exceeding man's belief, repeat;
Which therefore cannot be accounted lies,
For human wit could never such devise.
Some future truths are mingled in his book;
But where the witness fail'd, the prophet spoke: 655
Some things like visionary flights appear;
The spirit caught him up, the Lord knows where;

56

And gave him his rabbinical degree,
Unknown to foreign university.
His judgment yet his mem'ry did excel;   660
Which piec'd his wondrous evidence so well,
And suited to the temper of the times,
Then groaning under Jebusitic crimes.
Let Israel's foes suspect his heav'nly call,
And rashly judge his writ apocryphal;   665
Our laws for such affronts have forfeits made:
He takes his life, who takes away his trade.
Were I myself in witness Corah's place,
The wretch who did me such a dire disgrace,
Should whet my memory, tho' once forgot,   670
To make him an appendix of my plot.
His zeal to Heav'n made him his prince despise,
And load his person with indignities;
But zeal peculiar privilege affords,
Indulging latitude to deeds and words;   675
And Corah might for Agag's murther call,
In terms as coarse as Samuel us'd to Saul.
What others in his evidence did join,
(The best that could be had for love or coin,)
In Corah's own predicament will fall;   680
For *witness* is a common name to all.

  Surrounded thus with friends of every sort,
Deluded Absalom forsakes the court;
Impatient of high hopes, urg'd with renown,
And fir'd with near possession of a crown.   685
Th' admiring crowd are dazzled with surprise,
And on his goodly person feed their eyes.
His joy conceal'd, he sets himself to show,
On each side bowing popularly low;
His looks, his gestures, and his words he frames,   690
And with familiar ease repeats their names.
Thus form'd by nature, furnish'd out with arts,

He glides unfelt into their secret hearts.
Then, with a kind compassionating look,
And sighs, bespeaking pity ere he spoke,   695
Few words he said; but easy those and fit,
More slow than Hybla-drops, and far more sweet.

"I mourn, my countrymen, your lost estate;
Tho' far unable to prevent your fate:
Behold a banish'd man, for your dear cause   700
Expos'd a prey to arbitrary laws!
Yet O! that I alone could be undone,
Cut off from empire, and no more a son!
Now all your liberties a spoil are made;
Egypt and Tyrus intercept your trade,   705
And Jebusites your sacred rites invade.
My father, whom with reverence yet I name,
Charm'd into ease, is careless of his fame;
And, brib'd with petty sums of foreign gold,
Is grown in Bathsheba's embraces old;   710
Exalts his enemies, his friends destroys;
And all his pow'r against himself imploys.
He gives, and let him give, my right away;
But why should he his own and yours betray?
He, only he, can make the nation bleed,   715
And he alone from my revenge is freed.
Take then my tears, (with that he wip'd his eyes,)
'T is all the aid my present pow'r supplies:
No court-informer can these arms accuse;
These arms may sons against their fathers use: 720
And 't is my wish, the next successor's reign
May make no other Israelite complain."

Youth, beauty, graceful action seldom fail;
But common interest always will prevail;
And pity never ceases to be shown   725
To him who makes the people's wrongs his own.
The crowd, that still believe their kings oppress,

With lifted hands their young Messiah bless:
Who now begins his progress to ordain
With chariots, horsemen, and a num'rous train;   730
From east to west his glories he displays,
And, like the sun, the promis'd land surveys.
Fame runs before him as the morning star,
And shouts of joy salute him from afar:
Each house receives him as a guardian god,   735
And consecrates the place of his abode.
But hospitable treats did most commend
Wise Issachar, his wealthy western friend.
This moving court, that caught the people's eyes,
And seem'd but pomp, did other ends disguise: 740
Achitophel had form'd it, with intent
To sound the depths, and fathom, where it went,
The people's hearts; distinguish friends from foes,
And try their strength, before they came to blows.
Yet all was color'd with a smooth pretence   745
Of specious love, and duty to their prince.
Religion, and redress of grievances,
Two names that always cheat and always please,
Are often urg'd; and good King David's life
Endanger'd by a brother and a wife.   750
Thus in a pageant shew a plot is made,
And peace itself is war in masquerade.
O foolish Israel! never warn'd by ill!
Still the same bait, and circumvented still!
Did ever men forsake their present ease,   755
In midst of health imagine a disease;
Take pains contingent mischiefs to foresee,
Make heirs for monarchs, and for God decree?
What shall we think! Can people give away,
Both for themselves and sons, their native sway?   760
Then they are left defenceless to the sword
Of each unbounded, arbitrary lord:

And laws are vain, by which we right enjoy,
If kings unquestion'd can those laws destroy.
Yet if the crowd be judge of fit and just,   765
And kings are only officers in trust,
Then this resuming cov'nant was declar'd
When kings were made, or is for ever barr'd.
If those who gave the sceptre could not tie
By their own deed their own posterity,   770
How then could Adam bind his future race?
How could his forfeit on mankind take place?
Or how could heavenly justice damn us all,
Who ne'er consented to our father's fall?
Then kings are slaves to those whom they command,   775
And tenants to their people's pleasure stand.
Add, that the pow'r for property allow'd
Is mischievously seated in the crowd;
For who can be secure of private right,
If sovereign sway may be dissolv'd by might?   780
Nor is the people's judgment always true:
The most may err as grossly as the few;
And faultless kings run down, by common cry,
For vice, oppression, and for tyranny.
What standard is there in a fickle rout,   785
Which, flowing to the mark, runs faster out?
Nor only crowds, but Sanhedrins may be
Infected with this public lunacy,
And share the madness of rebellious times,
To murther monarchs for imagin'd crimes.   790
If they may give and take whene'er they please,
Not kings alone, (the godhead's images,)
But government itself at length must fall
To nature's state, where all have right to all.
Yet, grant our lords the people kings can make,   795
What prudent men a settled throne would shake?
For whatsoe'er their sufferings were before,

That change they covet makes them suffer more.
All other errors but disturb a state,
But innovation is the blow of fate.   800
If ancient fabrics nod, and threat to fall,
To patch the flaws, and buttress up the wall,
Thus far 't is duty: but here fix the mark;
For all beyond it is to touch our ark.
To change foundations, cast the frame anew,   805
Is work for rebels, who base ends pursue,
At once divine and human laws control,
And mend the parts by ruin of the whole.
The tamp'ring world is subject to this curse,
To physic their disease into a worse.   810
    Now what relief can righteous David bring?
How fatal 't is to be too good a king!
Friends he has few, so high the madness grows:
Who dare be such, must be the people's foes.
Yet some there were, ev'n in the worst of days;   815
Some let me name, and naming is to praise.
    In this short file Barzillai first appears;
Barzillai, crown'd with honour and with years.
Long since, the rising rebels he withstood
In regions waste, beyond the Jordan's flood: 820
Unfortunately brave to buoy the State;
But sinking underneath his master's fate:
In exile with his godlike prince he mourn'd;
For him he suffer'd, and with him return'd.
The court he practis'd, not the courtier's art: 825
Large was his wealth, but larger was his heart,
Which well the noblest objects knew to choose,
The fighting warrior, and recording Muse.
His bed could once a fruitful issue boast:
Now more than half a father's name is lost.   830
His eldest hope, with every grace adorn'd,
By me (so Heav'n will have it) always mourn'd,

61

And always honour'd, snatch'd in manhood's prime
B' unequal fates, and Providence's crime;
Yet not before the goal of honour won,   835
All parts fulfill'd of subject and of son:
Swift was the race, but short the time to run.
O narrow circle, but of pow'r divine,
Scanted in space, but perfect in thy line!
By sea, by land, thy matchless worth was known,   840
Arms thy delight, and war was all thy own:
Thy force, infus'd, the fainting Tyrians propp'd;
And haughty Pharaoh found his fortune stopp'd.
O ancient honour! O unconquer'd hand,
Whom foes unpunish'd never could withstand!   845
But Israel was unworthy of thy name;
Short is the date of all immoderate fame.
It looks as Heav'n our ruin had design'd,
And durst not trust thy fortune and thy mind.
Now, free from earth, thy disencumber'd soul   850
Mounts up, and leaves behind the clouds and starry pole:
From thence thy kindred legions mayst thou bring,
To aid the guardian angel of thy king.
Here stop, my Muse, here cease thy painful flight;
No pinions can pursue immortal height: 855
Tell good Barzillai thou canst sing no more,
And tell thy soul she should have fled before.
Or fled she with his life, and left this verse
To hang on her departed patron's hearse?
Now take thy steepy flight from heav'n, and see   860
If thou canst find on earth another *he*:
Another *he* would be too hard to find;
See then whom thou canst see not far behind.
Zadoc the priest, whom, shunning pow'r and place,
His lowly mind advanc'd to David's grace.   865
With him the Sagan of Jerusalem,
Of hospitable soul, and noble stem;

Him of the western dome, whose weighty sense
Flows in fit words and heavenly eloquence.
The prophets' sons, by such example led,   870
To learning and to loyalty were bred:
For colleges on bounteous kings depend,
And never rebel was to arts a friend.
To these succeed the pillars of the laws;
Who best could plead, and best can judge a cause. 875
Next them a train of loyal peers ascend;
Sharp-judging Adriel, the Muses' friend;
Himself a Muse — in Sanhedrin's debate
True to his prince, but not a slave of state:
Whom David's love with honours did adorn,   880
That from his disobedient son were torn.
Jotham of piercing wit, and pregnant thought;
Endued by nature, and by learning taught
To move assemblies, who but only tried
The worse a while, then chose the better side: 885
Nor chose alone, but turn'd the balance too;
So much the weight of one brave man can do.
Hushai, the friend of David in distress;
In public storms, of manly steadfastness:
By foreign treaties he inform'd his youth,   890
And join'd experience to his native truth.
His frugal care supplies the wanting throne;
Frugal for that, but bounteous of his own:
'T is easy conduct when exchequers flow,
But hard the task to manage well the low;   895
For sovereign power is too depress'd or high,
When kings are forc'd to sell, or crowds to buy.
Indulge one labour more, my weary Muse,
For Amiel: who can Amiel's praise refuse?
Of ancient race by birth, but nobler yet   900
In his own worth, and without title great:
The Sanhedrin long time as chief he rul'd,

Their reason guided, and their passion cool'd:
So dext'rous was he in the crown's defence,
So form'd to speak a loyal nation's sense,   905
That, as their band was Israel's tribes in small,
So fit was he to represent them all.
Now rasher charioteers the seat ascend,
Whose loose careers his steady skill commend:
They, like th' unequal ruler of the day,   910
Misguide the seasons, and mistake the way;
While he withdrawn at their mad labour smiles,
And safe enjoys the sabbath of his toils.

These were the chief, a small but faithful band
Of worthies, in the breach who dar'd to stand,   915
And tempt th' united fury of the land.
With grief they view'd such powerful engines bent,
To batter down the lawful government:
A numerous faction, with pretended frights,
In Sanhedrins to plume the regal rights;   920
The true successor from the court remov'd;
The Plot, by hireling witnesses, improv'd.
These ills they saw, and, as their duty bound,
They shew'd the king the danger of the wound;
That no concessions from the throne would please,   925
But lenitives fomented the disease;
That Absalom, ambitious of the crown,
Was made the lure to draw the people down;
That false Achitophel's pernicious hate
Had turn'd the Plot to ruin Church and State;   930
The council violent, the rabble worse;
That Shimei taught Jerusalem to curse.

With all these loads of injuries oppress'd,
And long revolving in his careful breast
Th' event of things, at last, his patience tir'd,   935
Thus from his royal throne, by Heav'n inspir'd,
The godlike David spoke: with awful fear

His train their Maker in their master hear.

    "Thus long have I, by native mercy sway'd,
My wrongs dissembled, my revenge delay'd: 940
So willing to forgive th' offending age;
So much the father did the king assuage.
But now so far my clemency they slight,
Th' offenders question my forgiving right.
That one was made for many, they contend;   945
But 't is to rule; for that 's a monarch's end.
They call my tenderness of blood, my fear;
Tho' manly tempers can the longest bear.
Yet, since they will divert my native course,
'T is time to shew I am not good by force.   950
Those heap'd affronts that haughty subjects bring,
Are burthens for a camel, not a king.
Kings are the public pillars of the State,
Born to sustain and prop the nation's weight;
If my young Samson will pretend a call   955
To shake the column, let him share the fall:
But O that yet he would repent and live!
How easy 't is for parents to forgive!
With how few tears a pardon might be won
From nature, pleading for a darling son!   960
Poor pitied youth, by my paternal care
Rais'd up to all the height his frame could bear!
Had God ordain'd his fate for empire born,
He would have giv'n his soul another turn:
Gull'd with a patriot's name, whose modern sense   965
Is one that would by law supplant his prince;
The people's brave, the politician's tool;
Never was patriot yet, but was a fool.
Whence comes it that religion and the laws
Should more be Absalom's than David's cause?   970
His old instructor, ere he lost his place,
Was never thought indued with so much grace.

Good heav'ns, how faction can a patriot paint!
My rebel ever proves my people's saint.
Would *they* impose an heir upon the throne?   975
Let Sanhedrins be taught to give their own.
A king's at least a part of government,
And mine as requisite as their consent;
Without my leave a future king to choose,
Infers a right the present to depose.   980
True, they petition me t' approve their choice;
But Esau's hands suit ill with Jacob's voice.
My pious subjects for my safety pray;
Which to secure, they take my pow'r away.
From plots and treasons Heav'n preserve my years,   985
But save me most from my petitioners!
Unsatiate as the barren womb or grave;
God cannot grant so much as they can crave.
What then is left, but with a jealous eye
To guard the small remains of royalty?   990
The law shall still direct my peaceful sway,
And the same law teach rebels to obey:
Votes shall no more establish'd pow'r control —
Such votes as make a part exceed the whole:
No groundless clamours shall my friends remove,   995
Nor crowds have pow'r to punish ere they prove;
For gods and godlike kings their care express,
Still to defend their servants in distress.
O that my pow'r to saving were confin'd!
Why am I forc'd, like Heav'n, against my mind,   1000
To make examples of another kind?
Must I at length the sword of justice draw?
O curst effects of necessary law!
How ill my fear they by my mercy scan!
Beware the fury of a patient man.   1005
Law they require, let Law then shew her face;
They could not be content to look on Grace,

Her hinder parts, but with a daring eye   1010
To tempt the terror of her front and die.
By their own arts, 't is righteously decreed,
Those dire artificers of death shall bleed.
Against themselves their witnesses will swear,
Till viper-like their mother Plot they tear;
And suck for nutriment that bloody gore,
Which was their principle of life before.   1015
Their Belial with their Belzebub will fight;
Thus on my foes, my foes shall do me right.
Nor doubt th' event; for factious crowds engage,
In their first onset, all their brutal rage.
Then let 'em take an unresisted course;   1020
Retire, and traverse, and delude their force;
But, when they stand all breathless, urge the fight,
And rise upon 'em with redoubled might;
For lawful pow'r is still superior found;
When long driv'n back, at length it stands the ground." 1025
  He said. Th' Almighty, nodding, gave consent;
And peals of thunder shook the firmament.
Henceforth a series of new time began,
The mighty years in long procession ran:
Once more, the godlike David was restor'd,   1030
And willing nations knew their lawful lord.

Extract from

The Medal

ALMIGHTY crowd, thou shorten'st all dispute;
Pow'r is thy essence, wit thy attribute!
Nor faith nor reason make thee at a stay,
Thou leap'st o'er all eternal truths in thy Pindaric way!
Athens no doubt did righteously decide,   95
When Phocion and when Socrates were tried;
As righteously they did those dooms repent;
Still they were wise, whatever way they went.
Crowds err not, tho' to both extremes they run;
To kill the father and recall the son.   100
Some think the fools were most, as times went then;
But now the world's o'erstock'd with prudent men.
The common cry is ev'n religion's test:
The Turk's is at Constantinople best;
Idols in India; Popery at Rome;   105
And our own worship only true at home.
And true, but for the time; 't is hard to know
How long we please it shall continue so.
This side to-day, and that to-morrow burns;
So all are God-a'mighties in their turns.   110
A tempting doctrine, plausible and new:
What fools our fathers were, if this be true!
Who, to destroy the seeds of civil war,
Inherent right in monarchs did declare;
And, that a lawful pow'r might never cease,   115
Secur'd succession, to secure our peace.
Thus property and sovereign sway, at last,
In equal balances, were justly cast:

But this new Jehu spurs the hot-mouth'd horse;
Instructs the beast to know his native force,   120
To take the bit between his teeth, and fly
To the next headlong steep of anarchy.
Too happy England, if our good we knew,
Would we possess the freedom we pursue!
The lavish government can give no more;   125
Yet we repine, and plenty makes us poor.
God tried us once: our rebel fathers fought;
He glutted 'em with all the pow'r they sought:
Till, master'd by their own usurping brave,
The freeborn subject sunk into a slave.   130
We loathe our manna, and we long for quails;
Ah, what is man, when his own wish prevails!
How rash, how swift to plunge himself in ill;
Proud of his pow'r, and boundless in his will!
That kings can do no wrong we must believe;   135
None can they do, and must they all receive?
Help, Heaven! or sadly we shall see an hour,
When neither wrong nor right are in their pow'r!
Already they have lost their best defence,
The benefit of laws which they dispense: 140
No justice to their righteous cause allow'd;
But baffled by an arbitrary crowd;
And medals grav'd, their conquest to record,
The stamp and coin of their adopted lord.

Macflecknoe

or, A Satire upon the True-Blue-Protestant Poet T. S.
By the author of Absalom and Achitophel

ALL human things are subject to decay,
And when fate summons, monarchs must obey.
This Flecknoe found, who, like Augustus, young
Was call'd to empire, and had govern'd long;
In prose and verse, was own'd, without dispute,   5
Thro' all the realms of *Nonsense*, absolute.
This aged prince, now flourishing in peace,
And blest with issue of a large increase;
Worn out with business, did at length debate
To settle the succession of the State;   10
And, pond'ring which of all his sons was fit
To reign, and wage immortal war with wit,
Cried: " 'T is resolv'd; for nature pleads, that he
Should only rule, who most resembles me.
Sh—— alone my perfect image bears,   15
Mature in dullness from his tender years:
Sh—— alone, of all my sons, is he
Who stands confirm'd in full stupidity.
The rest to some faint meaning make pretence,
But Sh—— never deviates into sense.   20
Some beams of wit on other souls may fall,
Strike thro', and make a lucid interval;
But Sh——'s genuine night admits no ray,
His rising fogs prevail upon the day.
Besides, his goodly fabric fills the eye,   25
And seems design'd for thoughtless majesty;
Thoughtless as monarch oaks that shade the plain,
And, spread in solemn state, supinely reign.

Heywood and Shirley were but types of thee,
Thou last great prophet of tautology.   30
Even I, a dunce of more renown than they,
Was sent before but to prepare thy way;
And, coarsely clad in Norwich drugget, came
To teach the nations in thy greater name.
My warbling lute, the lute I whilom strung,   35
When to King John of Portugal I sung,
Was but the prelude to that glorious day,
When thou on silver Thames didst cut thy way,
With well-tim'd oars before the royal barge,
Swell'd with the pride of thy celestial charge;   40
And big with hymn, commander of a host,
The like was ne'er in Epsom blankets toss'd.
Methinks I see the new Arion sail,
The lute still trembling underneath thy nail.
At thy well-sharpen'd thumb from shore to shore   45
The treble squeaks for fear, the basses roar;
Echoes from Pissing Alley Sh—— call,
And Sh—— they resound from Aston Hall.
About thy boat the little fishes throng,
As at the morning toast that floats along.   50
Sometimes, as prince of thy harmonious band,
Thou wield'st thy papers in thy threshing hand.
St André's feet ne'er kept more equal time,
Not ev'n the feet of thy own *Psyche's* rhyme;
Tho' they in number as in sense excel: 55
So just, so like tautology, they fell,
That, pale with envy, Singleton forswore
The lute and sword, which he in triumph bore,
And vow'd he ne'er would act Villerius more."
Here stopp'd the good old sire, and wept for joy   60
In silent raptures of the hopeful boy.
All arguments, but most his plays, persuade,
That for anointed dullness he was made.

Close to the walls which fair Augusta bind,
(The fair Augusta much to fears inclin'd,)   65
An ancient fabric rais'd t' inform the sight,
There stood of yore, and Barbican it hight:
A watchtower once; but now, so fate ordains,
Of all the pile an empty name remains.
From its old ruins brothel-houses rise,   70
Scenes of lewd loves, and of polluted joys,
Where their vast courts the mother-strumpets keep,
And, undisturb'd by watch, in silence sleep.
Near these a Nursery erects its head,
Where queens are form'd, and future heroes bred;   75
Where unfledg'd actors learn to laugh and cry,
Where infant punks their tender voices try,
And little Maximins the gods defy.
Great Fletcher never treads in buskins here,
Nor greater Jonson dares in socks appear;   80
But gentle Simkin just reception finds
Amidst this monument of vanish'd minds:
Pure clinches the suburbian Muse affords,
And Panton waging harmless war with words.
Here Flecknoe, as a place to fame well known,   85
Ambitiously design'd his Sh——'s throne;
For ancient Dekker prophesied long since,
That in this pile should reign a mighty prince,
Born for a scourge of wit, and flail of sense;
To whom true dullness should some *Psyches* owe,   90
But worlds of *Misers* from his pen should flow;
Humorists and *Hypocrites* it should produce,
Whole Raymond families, and tribes of Bruce.
   Now Empress Fame had publish'd the renown
Of Sh——'s coronation thro' the town.   95
Rous'd by report of Fame, the nations meet,
From near Bunhill, and distant Watling Street.
No Persian carpets spread th' imperial way,

But scatter'd limbs of mangled poets lay;
From dusty shops neglected authors come,   100
Martyrs of pies, and relics of the bum.
Much Heywood, Shirley, Ogleby there lay,
But loads of Sh—— almost chok'd the way.
Bilk'd stationers for yeoman stood prepar'd,
And Herringman was captain of the guard.   105
The hoary prince in majesty appear'd,
High on a throne of his own labours rear'd.
At his right hand our young Ascanius sate,
Rome's other hope, and pillar of the State.
His brows thick fogs, instead of glories, grace,   110
And lambent dullness play'd around his face.
As Hannibal did to the altars come,
Sworn by his sire a mortal foe to Rome;
So Sh—— swore, nor should his vow be vain,
That he till death true dullness would maintain;   115
And, in his father's right, and realm's defence,
Ne'er to have peace with wit, nor truce with sense.
The king himself the sacred unction made,
As king by office, and as priest by trade.
In his sinister hand, instead of ball,   120
He plac'd a mighty mug of potent ale;
Love's Kingdom to his right he did convey,
At once his sceptre, and his rule of sway;
Whose righteous lore the prince had practis'd young,
And from whose loins recorded *Psyche* sprung.   125
His temples, last, with poppies were o'erspread,
That nodding seem'd to consecrate his head.
Just at that point of time, if fame not lie,
On his left hand twelve reverend owls did fly.
So Romulus, 't is sung, by Tiber's brook,   130
Presage of sway from twice six vultures took.
Th' admiring throng loud acclamations make,
And omens of his future empire take.

The sire then shook the honours of his head,
And from his brows damps of oblivion shed   135
Full on the filial dullness: long he stood,
Repelling from his breast the raging god;
At length burst out in this prophetic mood:
"Heavens bless my son, from Ireland let him reign
To far Barbadoes on the western main;   140
Of his dominion may no end be known,
And greater than his father's be his throne;
Beyond *Love's Kingdom* let him stretch his pen!"
He paus'd, and all the people cried, "Amen."
Then thus continued he: "My son, advance   145
Still in new impudence, new ignorance.
Success let others teach, learn thou from me
Pangs without birth, and fruitless industry.
Let *Virtuosos* in five years be writ;
Yet not one thought accuse thy toil of wit.   150
Let gentle George in triumph tread the stage,
Make Dorimant betray, and Loveit rage;
Let Cully, Cockwood, Fopling, charm the pit,
And in their folly shew the writer's wit.
Yet still thy fools shall stand in thy defence,   155
And justify their author's want of sense.
Let 'em be all by thy own model made
Of dullness, and desire no foreign aid;
That they to future ages may be known,
Not copies drawn, but issue of thy own.   160
Nay, let thy men of wit too be the same,
All full of thee, and differing but in name.
But let no alien S—dl—y interpose,
To lard with wit thy hungry *Epsom* prose.
And when false flowers of rhetoric thou wouldst cull, 165
Trust nature, do not labour to be dull;
But write thy best, and top; and, in each line,
Sir Formal's oratory will be thine:

Sir Formal, tho' unsought, attends thy quill,
And does thy northern dedications fill.   170
Nor let false friends seduce thy mind to fame,
By arrogating Jonson's hostile name.
Let father Flecknoe fire thy mind with praise,
And uncle Ogleby thy envy raise.
Thou art my blood, where Jonson has no part: 175
What share have we in nature, or in art?
Where did his wit on learning fix a brand,
And rail at arts he did not understand?
Where made he love in Prince Nicander's vein,
Or swept the dust in *Psyche's* humble strain?   180
Where sold he bargains, 'whip-stitch, kiss my arse,'
Promis'd a play and dwindled to a farce?
When did his Muse from Fletcher scenes purloin,
As thou whole Eth'rege dost transfuse to thine?
But so transfus'd, as oil on water's flow,   185
His always floats above, thine sinks below.
This is thy province, this thy wondrous way,
New humours to invent for each new play:
This is that boasted bias of thy mind,
By which one way, to dullness, 't is inclin'd;   190
Which makes thy writings lean on one side still,
And, in all changes, that way bends thy will.
Nor let thy mountain-belly make pretence
Of likeness; thine 's a tympany of sense.
A tun of man in thy large bulk is writ,   195
But sure thou 'rt but a kilderkin of wit.
Like mine, thy gentle numbers feebly creep;
Thy tragic Muse gives smiles, thy comic sleep.
With whate'er gall thou sett'st thyself to write,
Thy inoffensive satires never bite.   200
In thy felonious heart tho' venom lies,
It does but touch thy Irish pen, and dies.
Thy genius calls thee not to purchase fame

In keen iambics, but mild anagram.
Leave writing plays, and choose for thy command   205
Some peaceful province in acrostic land.
There thou may'st wings display and altars raise,
And torture one poor word ten thousand ways.
Or, if thou wouldst thy diff'rent talents suit,
Set thy own songs, and sing them to thy lute."   210
    He said: but his last words were scarcely heard;
For Bruce and Longvil had a trap prepar'd,
And down they sent the yet declaiming bard.
Sinking he left his drugget robe behind,
Borne upwards by a subterranean wind.   215
The mantle fell to the young prophet's part,
With double portion of his father's art.

Extract from

Absalom and Achitophel

PART TWO

NEXT these, a troop of busy spirits press,   310
Of little fortunes, and of conscience less;
With them the tribe whose luxury had drain'd
Their banks, in former sequestrations gain'd:
Who rich and great by past rebellions grew,
And long to fish the troubled streams anew.   315
Some future hopes, some present payment draws,
To sell their conscience and espouse the cause,
Such stipends those vile hirelings best befit,
Priests without grace, and poets without wit.
Shall that false Hebronite escape our curse,   320
Judas that keeps the rebels' pension-purse;

Judas that pays the treason-writer's fee,
Judas that well deserves his namesake's tree;
Who at Jerusalem's own gates erects
His college for a nursery of sects.   325
Young prophets with an early care secures,
And with the dung of his own arts manures.
What have the men of Hebron here to do?
What part in Israel's promis'd land have you?
Here Phaleg the lay Hebronite is come,   330
'Cause like the rest he could not live at home;
Who from his own possessions cou'd not drain
An Omer even of Hebronitish grain,
Here struts it like a patriot, and talks high
Of injur'd subjects, alter'd property: 335
An emblem of that buzzing insect just,
That mounts the wheel, and thinks she raises dust.
Can dry bones live? Or skeletons produce
The vital warmth of cuckoldizing juice?
Slim Phaleg cou'd, and at the table fed,   340
Return'd the grateful product to the bed.
A waiting-man to trav'ling nobles chose,
He his own laws wou'd saucily impose;
Till bastinado'd back again he went,
To learn those manners he to teach was sent.   345
Chastiz'd, he ought to have retreated home,
But he reads politics to Absalom.
For never Hebronite though kicked and scorn'd,
To his own country willingly return'd.
    But leaving famish'd Phaleg to be fed,   350
And to talk treason for his daily bread,
Let Hebron, nay let hell produce a man
So made for mischief as Ben-Jochanan.
A Jew of humble parentage was he,
By trade a Levite though of low degree: 355
His pride no higher than the desk aspir'd,

77

But for the drudgery of priests was hir'd
To read and pray in linen ephod brave,
And pick up single shekels from the grave.
Married at last, and finding charge come faster,   360
He cou'd not live by God, but changed his master:
Inspir'd by want was made a factious tool,
They got a villain, and we lost a fool.
Still violent whatever cause he took,
But most against the party he forsook,   365
For renegadoes who ne'er turn by halves
Are bound in conscience to be double knaves.
So this prose-prophet took most monstrous pains
To let his masters see he earn'd his gains.
But as the Devil owes all his imps a shame,   370
He chose th' Apostate for his proper theme;
With little pains he made the picture true,
And from reflection took the rogue he drew.
A wondrous work to prove the Jewish nation
In every age a murmuring generation;   375
To trace 'em from their infancy of sinning,
And show 'em factious from their first beginning.
To prove they could rebel, and rail, and mock,
Much to the credit of the chosen flock;
A strong authority which must convince   380
That saints owe no allegiance to their prince.
As 'tis a leading-card to make a whore
To prove her mother had turned up before.
But tell me, did the drunken patriarch bless
The son that shew'd his father's nakedness?   385
Such thanks the present church thy pen will give,
Which proves rebellion was so primitive.
Must ancient failings be examples made?
Then murtherers from Cain may learn their trade.
As thou the heathen and the saint hast drawn,   390
Methinks th' Apostate was the better man:

78

And thy hot father (waiving my respect)
Not of a mother church, but of a sect.
And such he needs must be of thy indicting,
This comes of drinking asses' milk, and writing. 395
If Balak should be call'd to leave his place
(As profit is the loudest call of grace,)
His temple, dispossess'd of one, would be
Replenish'd with seven devils more by thee.

Levi, thou art a load, I'll lay thee down, 400
And shew Rebellion bare, without a gown;
Poor slaves in metre, dull and addle-pated,
Who rhyme below even David's psalms translated.
Some in my speedy pace I must outrun,
As lame Mephibosheth the wizard's son: 405
To make quick way I'll leap o'er heavy blocks,
Shun rotten Uzza as I wou'd the pox;
And hasten Og and Doeg to rehearse,
Two fools that crutch their feeble sense on verse;
Who by my muse to all succeeding times 410
Shall live in spite of their own doggerel rhymes.

Doeg, though without knowing how or why,
Made still a blundering kind of melody,
Spurr'd boldly on, and dashed through thick and thin,
Through sense and nonsense, never out nor in; 415
Free from all meaning, whether good or bad,
And in one word, heroically mad:

He was too warm on picking-work to dwell,
But faggoted his notions as they fell,
And if they rhymed and rattl'd all was well. 420
Spiteful he is not, though he wrote a satire,
For still there goes some thinking to ill-nature:
He needs no more than birds and beasts to think,
All his occasions are to eat and drink.
If he call rogue and rascal from a garret, 425
He means you no more mischief than a parrot:

The words for friend and foe alike were made,
To fetter 'em in verse is all his trade.
For almonds he'll cry 'Whore' to his own mother:
And call young Absalom King David's brother.   430
Let him be gallows-free by my consent,
And nothing suffer since he nothing meant;
Hanging supposes human soil and reason,
This animal's below committing treason:
Shall he be hang'd who never cou'd rebel?   435
That's a preferment for Achitophel.
The woman that committed buggery
Was rightly sentenc'd by the law to die;
But 'twas hard fate that to the gallows led
The dog that never heard the statute read.   440
Railing in other men may be a crime,
But ought to pass for mere instinct in him;
Instinct he follows and no farther knows,
For to write verse with him is to *transprose*.
'Twere pity treason at his door to lay,   445
Who makes Heaven's gate a lock to its own key:
Let him rail on, let his invective muse
Have four and twenty letters to abuse,
Which if he jumbles to one line of sense,
Indict him of a capital offence.   450
In fire-works give him leave to vent his spite,
Those are the only serpents he can write;
The height of his ambition is, we know,
But to be master of a puppet-show:
On that one stage his works may yet appear,   455
And a month's harvest keep bim all the year.

     Now stop your noses, Readers, all and some,
For here's a tun of midnight work to come,
Og from a treason-tavern rolling home.
Round as a globe, and liquor'd ev'ry chink,   460
Goodly and great he sails behind his link;

With all his bulk there's nothing lost in Og,
For ev'ry inch that is not fool is rogue:
A monstrous mass of foul corrupted matter,
As all the devils had spew'd to make the batter.   465
When wine has given him courage to blaspheme,
He curses God, but God before cursed him;
And if man cou'd have reason, none has more,
That made his paunch so rich and him so poor.
With wealth he was not trusted, for Heav'n knew   470
What 'twas of old to pamper up a Jew;
To what wou'd he on quail and pheasant swell,
That ev'n on tripe and carrion cou'd rebel?
But though Heav'n made him poor, (with rev'rence
    speaking,)
He never was a poet of God's making;   475
The midwife laid her hand on his thick skull,
With this prophetic blessing—Be thou dull!
Drink, swear and roar, forbear no lewd delight
Fit for thy bulk, do any thing but write:
Thou art of lasting make like thoughtless men,   480
A strong nativity—but for the pen;
Eat opium, mingle arsenic in thy drink,
Still thou mayst live avoiding pen and ink.
I see, I see 'tis counsel given in vain,
For treason botched in rhyme will be thy bane;   485
Rhyme is the rock on which thou art to wreck,
'Tis fatal to thy fame and to thy neck:
Why should thy metre good King David blast?
A psalm of his will surely be thy last.
Dar'st thou presume in verse to meet thy foes,   490
Thou whom the penny pamphlet foil'd in prose?
Doeg, whom God for mankind's mirth has made,
O'ertops thy talent in thy very trade;
Doeg to thee, thy paintings are so coarse,
A poet is, though he's the poets' horse.   495

A doubling noose thou on thy neck dost pull
For writing treason and for writing dull;
To die for faction is a common evil,
But to be hang'd for nonsense is the devil:
Had'st thou the glories of thy King express'd,   500
Thy praises had been satire at the best;
But thou in clumsy verse, unlicked, unpointed,
Hast shamefully defi'd the Lord's Anointed:
I will not rake the dunghill of thy crimes,
For who wou'd read thy life that reads thy rhymes?   505
But of King David's foes be this the doom,
May all be like the young man Absalom;
And for my foes, may this their blessing be,
To talk like Doeg, and to write like thee.

Extract from

Religio Laici

DIM as the borrow'd beams of moon and stars
To lonely, weary, wand'ring travellers,
Is Reason to the soul; and, as on high
Those rolling fires discover but the sky,
Not light us here, so Reason's glimmering ray   5
Was lent, not to assure our doubtful way,
But guide us upward to a better day.
And as those nightly tapers disappear,
When day's bright lord ascends our hemisphere;
So pale grows Reason at Religion's sight;   10
So dies, and so dissolves in supernatural light.
Some few, whose lamp shone brighter, have been led
From cause to cause, to nature's secret head;

And found that one first principle must be:
But what, or who, that UNIVERSAL HE;   15
Whether some soul incompassing this ball,
Unmade, unmov'd; yet making, moving all;
Or various atoms' interfering dance
Leapt into form, (the noble work of chance;)
Or this great all was from eternity;   20
Not ev'n the Stagirite himself could see,
And Epicurus guess'd as well as he:
As blindly grop'd they for a future state;
As rashly judg'd of providence and fate:
But least of all could their endeavours find   25
What most concern'd the good of humankind;
For happiness was never to be found,
But vanish'd from 'em like enchanted ground.
One thought content the good to be enjoy'd;
This every little accident destroy'd: 30
The wiser madmen did for virtue toil,
A thorny, or at best a barren soil;
In pleasure some their glutton souls would steep,
But found their line too short, the well too deep,
And leaky vessels which no bliss could keep.   35
Thus anxious thoughts in endless circles roll,
Without a centre where to fix the soul;
In this wild maze their vain endeavours end:
How can the less the greater comprehend?
Or finite reason reach Infinity?   40
For what could fathom GOD were more than He.

The Deist thinks he stands on firmer ground;
Cries: "Εὕρεκα, the mighty secret's found:
God is that spring of good; supreme and best;
We, made to serve, and in that service blest."   45
If so, some rules of worship must be given,
Distributed alike to all by Heaven:
Else God were partial, and to some denied

The means his justice should for all provide.
This general worship is to PRAISE and PRAY,   50
One part to borrow blessings, one to pay;
And when frail nature slides into offence,
The sacrifice for crimes is penitence.
Yet, since th' effects of providence, we find,
Are variously dispens'd to humankind;   55
That vice triumphs, and virtue suffers here,
(A brand that sovereign justice cannot bear;)
Our reason prompts us to a future state,
The last appeal from fortune and from fate:
Where God's all-righteous ways will be declar'd,   60
The bad meet punishment, the good reward.

　　Thus man by his own strength to heaven would soar,
And would not be oblig'd to God for more.
Vain, wretched creature, how art thou misled
To think thy wit these godlike notions bred!   65
These truths are not the product of thy mind,
But dropp'd from heaven, and of a nobler kind.
Reveal'd Religion first inform'd thy sight,
And Reason saw not, till Faith sprung the light.
Hence all thy natural worship takes the source: 70
'T is revelation what thou think'st discourse.
Else, how com'st thou to see these truths so clear,
Which so obscure to heathens did appear?
Not Plato these, nor Aristotle found;
Nor he whose wisdom oracles renown'd.   75
Hast thou a wit so deep, or so sublime,
Or canst thou lower dive, or higher climb?
Canst thou, by Reason, more of Godhead know
Than Plutarch, Seneca, or Cicero?
Those giant wits, in happier ages born,   80
(When arms and arts did Greece and Rome adorn,)
Knew no such system; no such piles could raise
Of natural worship, built on pray'r and praise,

To One Sole GOD:
Nor did remorse to expiate sin prescribe,   85
But slew their fellow creatures for a bribe:
The guiltless victim groan'd for their offence,
And cruelty and blood was penitence.
If sheep and oxen could atone for men,
Ah! at how cheap a rate the rich might sin!   90
And great oppressors might Heaven's wrath beguile,
By offering his own creatures for a spoil!

    Dar'st thou, poor worm, offend Infinity?
And must the terms of peace be given by thee?
Then thou art Justice in the last appeal: 95
Thy easy God instructs thee to rebel;
And, like a king remote, and weak, must take
What satisfaction thou art pleas'd to make.

    But if there be a pow'r too just and strong
To wink at crimes, and bear unpunish'd wrong;   100
Look humbly upward, see his will disclose
The forfeit first, and then the fine impose:
A mulct thy poverty could never pay,
Had not eternal wisdom found the way,
And with celestial wealth supplied thy store: 105
His justice makes the fine, his mercy quits the score.
See God descending in thy human frame;
Th' offended suff'ring in th' offender's name;
All thy misdeeds to him imputed see,
And all his righteousness devolv'd on thee.   110

    For granting we have sinn'd, and that th' offence
Of man is made against Omnipotence,
Some price that bears proportion must be paid,
And infinite with infinite be weigh'd.
See then the Deist lost: remorse for vice,   115
Not paid; or paid, inadequate in price:
What farther means can Reason now direct,
Or what relief from human wit expect?

That shews us sick; and sadly are we sure
Still to be sick, till Heav'n reveal the cure: 120
If then Heav'n's will must needs be understood,
(Which must, if we want cure, and Heaven be good,)
Let all records of will reveal'd be shown;
With Scripture all in equal balance thrown,
And our one sacred book will be that one.   125
  Proof needs not here, for whether we compare
That impious, idle, superstitious ware
Of rites, lustrations, offerings, (which before,
In various ages, various countries bore,)
With Christian faith and virtues, we shall find   130
None answ'ring the great ends of humankind,
But this one rule of life, that shews us best
How God may be appeas'd, and mortals blest.
Whether from length of time its worth we draw,
The world is scarce more ancient than the law: 135
Heav'n's early care prescrib'd for every age;
First, in the soul, and after, in the page.
Or, whether more abstractedly we look,
Or on the writers, or the written book,
Whence, but from heav'n, could men unskill'd in arts,   140
In several ages born, in several parts,
Weave such agreeing truths? or how, or why,
Should all conspire to cheat us with a lie?
Unask'd their pains, ungrateful their advice,
Starving their gain, and martyrdom their price.   145
  If on the book itself we cast our view,
Concurrent heathens prove the story true;
The doctrine, miracles; which must convince,
For Heav'n in them appeals to human sense:
And tho' they prove not, they confirm the cause,   150
When what is taught agrees with nature's laws.
  Then for the style; majestic and divine,
It speaks no less than God in every line:

Commanding words; whose force is still the same
As the first fiat that produc'd our frame. 155
All faiths beside or did by arms ascend,
Or sense indulg'd has made mankind their friend:
This only doctrine does our lusts oppose,
Unfed by nature's soil, in which it grows;
Cross to our interests, curbing sense and sin; 160
Oppress'd without, and undermin'd within,
It thrives thro' pain; its own tormentors tires;
And with a stubborn patience still aspires.
To what can Reason such effects assign,
Transcending nature, but to laws divine? 165
Which in that sacred volume are contain'd;
Sufficient, clear, and for that use ordain'd.

To the Memory of Mr Oldham

FAREWELL, too little, and too lately known,
Whom I began to think and call my own:
For sure our souls were near allied, and thine
Cast in the same poetic mould with mine.
One common note on either lyre did strike, 5
And knaves and fools we both abhorr'd alike.
To the same goal did both our studies drive;
The last set out the soonest did arrive.
Thus Nisus fell upon the slippery place,
While his young friend perform'd and won the race. 10
O early ripe! to thy abundant store
What could advancing age have added more?
It might (what nature never gives the young)
Have taught the numbers of thy native tongue.
But satire needs not those, and wit will shine 15
Thro' the harsh cadence of a rugged line:

A noble error, and but seldom made,
When poets are by too much force betray'd.
Thy generous fruits, tho' gather'd ere their prime,
Still shew'd a quickness; and maturing time   20
But mellows what we write to the dull sweets of rhyme.
Once more, hail and farewell; farewell, thou young,
But ah too short, Marcellus of our tongue;
Thy brows with ivy, and with laurels bound;
But fate and gloomy night encompass thee around.   25

A New Song

I

SYLVIA, the fair, in the bloom of fifteen,
Felt an innocent warmth as she lay on the green;
She had heard of a pleasure, and something she guess'd
By the towzing, and tumbling, and touching her breast.
She saw the men eager, but was at a loss,   5
What they meant by their sighing, and kissing so close;
    By their praying and whining,
    And clasping and twining,
    And panting and wishing,
    And sighing and kissing,   10
  And sighing and kissing so close.

II

"Ah!" she cried, "ah! for a languishing maid,
In a country of Christians, to die without aid!
Not a Whig, or a Tory, or Trimmer at least,
Or a Protestant parson, or Catholic priest,   15
To instruct a young virgin, that is at a loss,
What they meant by their sighing, and kissing so close!

By their praying and whining,
And clasping and twining,
And panting and wishing,   20
And sighing and kissing,
And sighing and kissing so close."

Cupid, in shape of a swain, did appear,
He saw the sad wound, and in pity drew near;
Then show'd her his arrow, and bid her not fear,   25
For the pain was no more than a maiden may bear.
When the balm was infus'd, she was not at a loss,
What they meant by their sighing, and kissing so close;
By their praying and whining,
And clasping and twining,   30
And panting and wishing,
And sighing and kissing,
And sighing and kissing so close.

To the Pious Memory of the accomplished Young Lady

Mrs Anne Killigrew

I

THOU youngest virgin-daughter of the skies,
Made in the last promotion of the blest;
Whose palms, new pluck'd from paradise,
In spreading branches more sublimely rise,
Rich with immortal green above the rest: 5
Whether, adopted to some neighbouring star,
Thou roll'st above us, in thy wand'ring race,
Or, in procession fix'd and regular,
Mov'd with the heavens' majestic pace;
Or, call'd to more superior bliss,   10

Thou tread'st, with seraphims, the vast abyss:
Whatever happy region is thy place,
Cease thy celestial song a little space;
(Thou wilt have time enough for hymns divine,
    Since heav'n's eternal year is thine.)   15
Hear then a mortal Muse thy praise rehearse,
       In no ignoble verse;
But such as thy own voice did practise here,
When thy first fruits of poesy were giv'n,
To make thyself a welcome inmate there;   20
    While yet a young probationer,
    And candidate of heav'n.

II

If by traduction came thy mind,
  Our wonder is the less to find
A soul so charming from a stock so good;   25
Thy father was transfus'd into thy blood:
So wert thou born into the tuneful strain,
(An early, rich, and inexhausted vein.)
    But if thy pre-existing soul   30
    Was form'd, at first, with myriads more,
It did thro' all the mighty poets roll,
    Who Greek or Latin laurels wore,
And was that Sappho last, which once it was before.
    If so, then cease thy flight, O *heav'n-born mind!*
    Thou hast no dross to purge from thy rich ore;   35
    Nor can thy soul a fairer mansion find,
    Than was the beauteous frame she left behind:
Return, to fill or mend the choir of thy celestial kind.

III

May we presume to say, that at thy birth
New joy was sprung in heav'n, as well as here on earth?   40
    For sure the milder planets did combine

On thy auspicious horoscope to shine,
And ev'n the most malicious were in trine.
Thy brother-angels at thy birth
    Strung each his lyre, and tun'd it high,   45
    That all the people of the sky
Might know a poetess was born on earth.
    And then, if ever, mortal ears
Had heard the music of the spheres!
And if no clust'ring swarm of bees   50
On thy sweet mouth distill'd their golden dew,
    'T was that such vulgar miracles
Heav'n had not leisure to renew:
For all the blest fraternity of love
Solemniz'd there thy birth, and kept thy holiday above.   55

IV

O gracious God! how far have we
Profan'd thy heav'nly gift of poesy!
Made prostitute and profligate the Muse,
Debas'd to each obscene and impious use,
Whose harmony was first ordain'd above   60
For tongues of angels, and for hymns of love!
O wretched we! why were we hurried down
    This lubric and adult'rate age,
(Nay, added fat pollutions of our own,)
    T' increase the steaming ordures of the stage?   65
What can we say t' excuse our *second fall*?
Let this thy *vestal*, Heav'n, atone for all:
Her Arethusian stream remains unsoil'd,
Unmix'd with foreign filth, and undefil'd;
Her wit was more than man, her innocence a child!   70

V

Art she had none, yet wanted none;
For nature did that want supply:

So rich in treasures of her own,
   She might our boasted stores defy:
Such noble vigour did her verse adorn   75
That it seem'd borrow'd, where 't was only born.
Her morals too were in her bosom bred,
   By great examples daily fed,
What in the best of books, her father's life, she read.
And to be read herself she need not fear;   80
Each test, and ev'ry light, her Muse will bear,
Tho' Epictetus with his lamp were there.
Ev'n love (for love sometimes her Muse express'd)
Was but a *lambent flame* which play'd about her breast,
Light as the vapours of a morning dream: 85
So cold herself, whilst she such warmth express'd,
'T was Cupid bathing in Diana's stream.

VI

Born to the spacious empire of the Nine,
One would have thought she should have been content
To manage well that mighty government;   90
But what can young ambitious souls confine?
   To the next realm she stretch'd her sway,
   For *painture* near adjoining lay,
A plenteous province, and alluring prey.
   A chamber of dependences was fram'd,   95
(As conquerors will never want pretence,
   When arm'd, to justify th' offence,)
And the whole fief in right of poetry she claim'd.
The country open lay without defence;
For poets frequent inroads there had made,   100
   And perfectly could represent
   The shape, the face, with ev'ry lineament;
And all the large demains which the *Dumb Sister* sway'd,
   All bow'd beneath her government;
   Receiv'd in triumph wheresoe'er she went.   105

Her pencil drew whate'er her soul design'd,
And oft the happy draught surpass'd the image in her mind.
    The *sylvan* scenes of herds and flocks,
    And fruitful plains and barren rocks,
    Of shallow brooks that flow'd so clear   110
    The bottom did the top appear;
    Of deeper too and ampler floods,
    Which, as in mirrors, shew'd the woods;
    Of lofty trees, with sacred shades,
    And perspectives of pleasant glades,   115
    Where nymphs of brightest form appear,
    And shaggy satyrs standing near,
    Which them at once admire and fear:
    The ruins too of some majestic piece,
    Boasting the pow'r of ancient Rome, or Greece,   120
    Whose statues, friezes, columns broken lie,
    And, tho' defac'd, the wonder of the eye:
    What nature, art, bold fiction, e'er durst frame,
    Her forming hand gave feature to the name.
    So strange a concourse ne'er was seen before,   125
But when the peopled ark the whole creation bore.

VII

    The scene then chang'd: with bold erected look
Our martial king the sight with reverence strook;
For, not content t' express his outward part,
Her hand call'd out the image of his heart: 130
His warlike mind, his soul devoid of fear,
His high-designing thoughts were figur'd there,
As when, by magic, ghosts are made appear.
    Our Phœnix queen was portray'd too so bright,
Beauty alone could beauty take so right: 135
Her dress, her shape, her matchless grace,
Were all observ'd, as well as heav'nly face.
With such a peerless majesty she stands,

93

As in that day she took the crown from sacred hands;
Before a train of heroines was seen,   140
In beauty foremost, as in rank the queen.
Thus nothing to her *genius* was denied,
  But like a ball of fire the further thrown,
    Still with a greater blaze she shone,
And her bright soul broke out on ev'ry side.   145
What next she had design'd, Heaven only knows;
  To such immod'rate growth her conquest rose
That fate alone its progress could oppose.

VIII

  Now all those charms, that blooming grace,
The well-proportion'd shape, and beauteous face,   150
Shall never more be seen by mortal eyes:
In earth the much-lamented virgin lies!
  Not wit, nor piety could fate prevent;
  Nor was the cruel Destiny content
    To finish all the murder at a blow,   155
  To sweep at once her life and beauty too;
But, like a harden'd felon, took a pride
    To work more mischievously slow,
And plunder'd first, and then destroy'd.
O double sacrilege on things divine,   160
  To rob the relic, and deface the shrine!
    But thus Orinda died:
Heav'n, by the same disease, did both translate;
As equal were their souls, so equal was their fate.

IX

Meantime her warlike brother on the seas   165
  His waving streamers to the winds displays,
And vows for his return, with vain devotion, pays.
    Ah, generous youth, that wish forbear,
    The winds too soon will waft thee here!

Slack all thy sails, and fear to come,   170
Alas, thou know'st not, thou art wreck'd at home!
No more shalt thou behold thy sister's face,
Thou hast already had her last embrace.
But look aloft, and if thou kenn'st from far
Among the Pleiads a new kindled star;   175
If any sparkles than the rest more bright,
'T is she that shines in that propitious light.

X

When in mid-air the golden trump shall sound,
    To raise the nations under ground;
    When in the Valley of Jehosaphat   180
The judging God shall close the book of fate,
        And there the last assizes keep
        For those who wake and those who sleep;
        When rattling bones together fly
        From the four corners of the sky;   185
When sinews o'er the skeletons are spread,
Those cloth'd with flesh, and life inspires the dead;
The sacred poets first shall hear the sound,
    And foremost from the tomb shall bound,
For they are cover'd with the lightest ground;   190
And straight, with inborn vigour, on the wing,
Like mounting larks, to the new morning sing.
There thou, sweet saint, before the choir shalt go,
As harbinger of heav'n, the way to show,
The way which thou so well hast learn'd below.   195

Extracts from

The Hind and the Panther

A MILK-WHITE Hind, immortal and unchang'd,
Fed on the lawns, and in the forest rang'd;
Without unspotted, innocent within,
She fear'd no danger, for she knew no sin.
Yet had she oft been chas'd with horns and hounds   5
And Scythian shafts; and many winged wounds
Aim'd at her heart; was often forc'd to fly,
And doom'd to death, tho' fated not to die.

   Not so her young; for their unequal line
Was hero's make, half human, half divine.   10
Their earthly mould obnoxious was to fate,
Th' immortal part assum'd immortal state.
Of these a slaughter'd army lay in blood,
Extended o'er the Caledonian wood,
Their native walk; whose vocal blood arose,   15
And cried for pardon on their perjur'd foes.
Their fate was fruitful, and the sanguine seed,
Endued with souls, encreas'd the sacred breed.
So captive Israel multiplied in chains,
A numerous exile, and enjoy'd her pains.   20
With grief and gladness mix'd, their mother view'd
Her martyr'd offspring, and their race renew'd;
Their crops to perish, but their kind to last,
So much the deathless plant the dying fruit surpass'd.

   Panting and pensive now she rang'd alone,   25
And wander'd in the kingdoms, once her own.

The common hunt, tho' from their rage restrain'd
By sov'reign pow'r, her company disdain'd;
Grinn'd as they pass'd, and with a glaring eye
Gave gloomy signs of secret enmity.   30
'T is true, she bounded by, and tripp'd so light,
They had not time to take a steady sight;
For Truth has such a face and such a mien,
As to be lov'd needs only to be seen.

The bloody Bear, an *Independent* beast,   35
Unlick'd to form, in groans her hate express'd.
Among the timorous kind the *Quaking* Hare
Profess'd neutrality, but would not swear.
Next her the *buffoon* Ape, as atheists use,
Mimick'd all sects, and had his own to choose: 40
Still when the Lion look'd, his knees he bent,
And paid at church a courtier's compliment.

The bristled *Baptist* Boar, impure as he,
(But whiten'd with the foam of sanctity,)
With fat pollutions fill'd the sacred place,   45
And mountains level'd in his furious race:
So first rebellion founded was in grace.
But since the mighty ravage which he made
In German forests had his guilt betray'd,
With broken tusks, and with a borrow'd name,   50
He shunn'd the vengeance, and conceal'd the shame;
So lurk'd in sects unseen. With greater guile
False Reynard fed on consecrated spoil:
The graceless beast by Athanasius first
Was chas'd from Nice; then, by Socinus nurs'd,   55
His impious race their blasphemy renew'd,
And nature's King thro' nature's optics view'd.
Revers'd, they view'd him lessen'd to their eye,
Nor in an infant could a God descry:
New swarming sects to this obliquely tend,   60
Hence they began, and here they all will end.

What weight of ancient witness can prevail,
If private reason hold the public scale?
But, gracious God, how well dost thou provide
For erring judgments an unerring guide!   65
Thy throne is darkness in th' abyss of light,
A blaze of glory that forbids the sight.
O teach me to believe thee thus conceal'd,
And search no farther than thyself reveal'd;
But her alone for my director take,   70
Whom thou hast promis'd never to forsake!
My thoughtless youth was wing'd with vain desires,
My manhood, long misled by wand'ring fires,
Follow'd false lights; and, when their glimpse was gone,
My pride struck out new sparkles of her own.   75
Such was I, such by nature still I am;
Be thine the glory, and be mine the shame.
Good life be now my task: my doubts are done:
(What more could fright my faith, than three in one?)
Can I believe eternal God could lie   80
Disguis'd in mortal mould and infancy?
That the great Maker of the world could die?
And after that trust my imperfect sense,
Which calls in question his omnipotence?
Can I my reason to my faith compel,   85
And shall my sight, and touch, and taste rebel?
Superior faculties are set aside;
Shall their subservient organs be my guide?
Then let the moon usurp the rule of day,
And winking tapers shew the sun his way;   90
For what my senses can themselves perceive,
I need no revelation to believe.
Can they who say the host should be descried
By sense, define a body glorified?
Impassible, and penetrating parts?   95
Let them declare by what mysterious arts

He shot that body thro' th' opposing might
Of bolts and bars impervious to the light,
And stood before his train confess'd in open sight.

*   *   *   *   *

The Panther, sure the noblest, next the Hind,
And fairest creature of the spotted kind;
O, could her inborn stains be wash'd away,
She were too good to be a beast of prey!   330
How can I praise, or blame, and not offend,
Or how divide the frailty from the friend!
Her faults and virtues lie so mix'd that she
Nor wholly stands condemn'd, nor wholly free.
Then, like her injur'd Lion, let me speak;   335
He cannot bend her, and he would not break.
Unkind already, and estrang'd in part,
The Wolf begins to share her wand'ring heart.
Tho' unpolluted yet with actual ill,
She half commits, who sins but in her will.   340
If, as our dreaming Platonists report,
There could be spirits of a middle sort,
Too black for heav'n, and yet too white for hell,
Who just dropp'd halfway down, nor lower fell;
So pois'd, so gently she descends from high,   345
It seems a soft dismission from the sky.

*   *   *   *   *

One evening, while the cooler shade she sought,
Revolving many a melancholy thought,
Alone she walk'd, and look'd around in vain,
With rueful visage, for her vanish'd train:
None of her sylvan subjects made their court;   515
Levées and couchées pass'd without resort.
So hardly can usurpers manage well
Those whom they first instructed to rebel:
More liberty begets desire of more;
The hunger still encreases with the store.   520

99

Without respect they brush'd along the wood,
Each in his clan, and, fill'd with loathsome food,
Ask'd no permission to the neighb'ring flood.
The Panther, full of inward discontent,
Since they would go, before 'em wisely went;   525
Supplying want of pow'r by drinking first,
As if she gave 'em leave to quench their thirst.
Among the rest, the Hind, with fearful face,
Beheld from far the common wat'ring place,
Nor durst approach; till with an awful roar   530
The sovereign Lion bade her fear no more.
Encourag'd thus she brought her younglings nigh,
Watching the motions of her patron's eye,
And drank a sober draught; the rest amaz'd
Stood mutely still, and on the stranger gaz'd;   535
Survey'd her part by part, and sought to find
The ten-horn'd monster in the harmless Hind,
Such as the Wolf and Panther had design'd.
They thought at first they dream'd; for 't was offence
With them to question certitude of sense,   540
Their guide in faith; but nearer when they drew,
And had the faultless object full in view,
Lord, how they all admir'd her heav'nly hue!
Some, who before her fellowship disdain'd,
Scarce, and but scarce, from inborn rage restrain'd, 545
Now frisk'd about her, and old kindred feign'd.
Whether for love or int'rest, ev'ry sect
Of all the salvage nation shew'd respect:
The viceroy Panther could not awe the herd;
The more the company, the less they fear'd.   550
The surly Wolf with secret envy burst,
Yet could not howl; the Hind had seen him first:
But what he durst not speak, the Panther durst.
    For when the herd, suffic'd, did late repair
To ferny heaths, and to their forest lair,   555

She made a mannerly excuse to stay,
Proff'ring the Hind to wait her half the way;
That, since the sky was clear, an hour of talk
Might help her to beguile the tedious walk.
With much good will the motion was embrac'd,   560
To chat a while on their adventures pass'd;
Nor had the grateful Hind so soon forgot
Her friend and fellow-suff'rer in the Plot.
Yet wond'ring how of late she grew estrang'd,
Her forehead cloudy, and her count'nance chang'd,   565
She thought this hour th' occasion would present
To learn her secret cause of discontent,
Which well she hop'd might be with ease redress'd,
Consid'ring her a well-bred civil beast,
And more a gentlewoman than the rest.   570
After some common talk what rumours ran,
The lady of the spotted muff began.

    *   *   *   *

    By this, the Hind had reach'd her lonely cell,   1235
And vapours rose, and dews unwholesome fell.
When she, by frequent observation wise,
As one who long on heav'n had fix'd her eyes,
Discern'd a change of weather in the skies.
The western borders were with crimson spread,   1240
The moon descending look'd all flaming red;
She thought good manners bound her to invite
The stranger dame to be her guest that night.
'T is true, coarse diet, and a short repast,
(She said,) were weak inducements to the taste   1245
Of one so nicely bred, and so unus'd to fast;
But what plain fare her cottage could afford,
A hearty welcome at a homely board,
Was freely hers; and, to supply the rest,
An honest meaning, and an open breast: 1250
Last, with content of mind, the poor man's wealth,

A grace cup to their common patron's health.
This she desir'd her to accept, and stay,
For fear she might be wilder'd in her way,
Because she wanted an unerring guide; 1255
And then the dewdrops on her silken hide
Her tender constitution did declare,
Too lady-like a long fatigue to bear,
And rough inclemencies of raw nocturnal air.
But most she fear'd that, travelling so late, 1260
Some evil-minded beasts might lie in wait,
And without witness wreak their hidden hate.

    The Panther, tho' she lent a list'ning ear,
Had more of Lion in her than to fear:
Yet wisely weighing, since she had to deal 1265
With many foes, their numbers might prevail,
Return'd her all the thanks she could afford,
And took her friendly hostess at her word;
Who, ent'ring first her lowly roof, (a shed
With hoary moss and winding ivy spread, 1270
Honest enough to hide an humble hermit's head,)
Thus graciously bespoke her welcome guest:
"So might these walls, with your fair presence blest,
Become your dwelling place of everlasting rest,
Not for a night, or quick revolving year; 1275
Welcome an owner, not a sojourner.
This peaceful seat my poverty secures;
War seldom enters but where wealth allures:
Nor yet despise it; for this poor abode
Has oft receiv'd, and yet receives a god; 1280
A god victorious of the Stygian race
Here laid his sacred limbs, and sanctified the place.
This mean retreat did mighty Pan contain:
Be emulous of him, and pomp disdain,
And dare not to debase your soul to gain." 1285
    The silent stranger stood amaz'd to see

Contempt of wealth, and wilful poverty;
And, tho' ill habits are not soon controll'd,
Awhile suspended her desire of gold;
But civilly drew in her sharpen'd paws,   1290
Not violating hospitable laws,
And pacified her tail, and lick'd her frothy jaws.
  The Hind did first her country cates provide;
Then couch'd herself securely by her side.

*   *   *   *   *

  "The Swallow, privileg'd above the rest
Of all the birds, as man's familiar guest,
Pursues the sun in summer brisk and bold,
But wisely shuns the persecuting cold:
Is well to chancels and to chimneys known,   1725
Tho' 't is not thought she feeds on smoke alone.
From hence she has been held of heav'nly line,
Endued with particles of soul divine.
This merry chorister had long possess'd
Her summer seat, and feather'd well her nest: 1730
Till frowning skies began to change their cheer,
And time turn'd up the wrong side of the year;
The shedding trees began the ground to strow
With yellow leaves, and bitter blasts to blow.
Sad auguries of winter thence she drew,   1735
Which by instinct, or prophecy, she knew:
When prudence warn'd her to remove betimes,
And seek a better heav'n and warmer climes.
  "Her sons were summon'd on a steeple's height,
And, call'd in common council, vote a flight;   1740
The day was nam'd, the next that should be fair;
All to the gen'ral rendezvous repair;
They try their flutt'ring wings, and trust themselves in air,
But whether upward to the moon they go,
Or dream the winter out in caves below,   1745
Or hawk at flies elsewhere, concerns not us to know.

"Southwards, you may be sure, they bent their flight,
And harbour'd in a hollow rock at night:
Next morn they rose, and set up ev'ry sail;
The wind was fair, but blew a *mack'rel* gale: 1750
The sickly young sat shiv'ring on the shore,
Abhorr'd salt water never seen before,
And pray'd their tender mothers to delay
The passage, and expect a fairer day.

*   *   *   *   *

"No longer doubting, all prepare to fly,   1855
And repossess their patrimonial sky.
The priest before 'em did his wings display;
And that good omens might attend their way.
As luck would have it, 't was St Martin's day.
"Who but the Swallow now triumphs alone?   1860
The canopy of heaven is all her own;
Her youthful offspring to their haunts repair,
And glide along in glades, and skim in air,
And dip for insects in the purling springs,
And stoop on rivers to refresh their wings.   1865
Their mothers think a fair provision made,
That ev'ry son can live upon his trade:
And, now the careful charge is off their hands,
Look out for husbands, and new nuptial bands:
The youthful widow longs to be supplied;   1870
But first the lover is by lawyers tied
To settle jointure-chimneys on the bride
So thick they couple, in so short a space,
That Martin's marriage-off'rings rise apace;
Their ancient houses, running to decay,   1875
Are furbish'd up, and cemented with clay:
They teem already; store of eggs are laid,
And brooding mothers call Lucina's aid.
Fame spreads the news, and foreign fowls appear
In flocks to greet the new returning year,   1880

104

To bless the founder, and partake the cheer.

"And now 't was time (so fast their numbers rise)
To plant abroad, and people colonies.
The youth drawn forth, as Martin had desir'd,
(For so their cruel destiny requir'd,)   1885
Were sent far off on an ill-fated day;
The rest would need conduct 'em on their way,
And Martin went, because he fear'd alone to stay.

"So long they flew with inconsiderate haste
That now their afternoon began to waste;   1890
And, what was ominous, that very morn
The sun was enter'd into Capricorn;
Which, by their bad astronomer's account,
That week the Virgin Balance should remount;
An infant moon eclips'd him in his way,   1895
And hid the small remainders of his day.
The crowd, amaz'd, pursued no certain mark;
But birds met birds, and justled in the dark:
Few mind the public in a panic fright;
And fear increas'd the horror of the night.   1900
Night came, but unattended with repose;
Alone she came, no sleep their eyes to close:
Alone, and black she came; no friendly stars arose.

"What should they do, beset with dangers round,
No neighb'ring dorp, no lodging to be found,   1905
But bleaky plains, and bare unhospitable ground.
The latter brood, who just began to fly,
Sick-feather'd, and unpractis'd in the sky,
For succour to their helpless mother call;
She spread her wings; some few beneath 'em crawl;   1910
She spread 'em wider yet, but could not cover all.
T' augment their woes, the winds began to move
Debate in air, for empty fields above,
Till Boreas got the skies, and pour'd amain
His rattling hailstones mix'd with snow and rain.   1915

105

"The joyless morning late arose, and found
A dreadful desolation reign around,
Some buried in the snow, some frozen to the ground.
The rest were struggling still with death, and lay,
The Crows' and Ravens' rights, an undefended prey: 1920
Excepting Martin's race; for they and he
Had gain'd the shelter of a hollow tree:
But, soon discover'd by a sturdy clown,
He headed all the rabble of a town,
And finish'd 'em with bats, or poll'd 'em down.   1925
Martin himself was caught alive, and tried
For treas'nous crimes, because the laws provide
No Martin there in winter shall abide.
High on an oak, which never leaf shall bear,
He breath'd his last, expos'd to open air;   1930
And there his corps, unblest, are hanging still,
To show the change of winds with his prophetic bill."

A Song for St Cecilia's Day, 1687

I

FROM harmony, from heav'nly harmony
    This universal frame began:
        When Nature underneath a heap
            Of jarring atoms lay,
            And could not heave her head,   5
The tuneful voice was heard from high:
        "Arise, ye more than dead."
Then cold, and hot, and moist, and dry,
    In order to their stations leap,
            And Music's pow'r obey.   10
From harmony, from heav'nly harmony

This universal frame began:
From harmony to harmony
Thro' all the compass of the notes it ran,
The diapason closing full in Man.   15

II

What passion cannot Music raise and quell!
When Jubal struck the corded shell,
His list'ning brethren stood around,
And, wond'ring, on their faces fell
To worship that celestial sound.   20
Less than a god they thought there could not dwell
Within the hollow of that shell
That spoke so sweetly and so well.
What passion cannot Music raise and quell!

III

The Trumpet's loud clangour   25
Excites us to arms,
With shrill notes of anger,
And mortal alarms.
The double double double beat
Of the thund'ring Drum   30
Cries: "Hark! the foes come;
Charge, charge, 't is too late to retreat."

IV

The soft complaining Flute
In dying notes discovers
The woes of hopeless lovers,   35
Whose dirge is whisper'd by the warbling Lute.

V

Sharp Violins proclaim
Their jealous pangs, and desperation,

Fury, frantic indignation,
Depth of pains, and height of passion,   40
    For the fair, disdainful dame.

VI

    But O! what art can teach,
    What human voice can reach,
The sacred Organ's praise?
    Notes inspiring holy love,   45
Notes that wing their heav'nly ways
    To mend the choirs above.

VII

Orpheus could lead the savage race;
And trees unrooted left their place,
    Sequacious of the lyre;   50
But bright Cecilia rais'd the wonder high'r:
When to her Organ vocal breath was giv'n,
    An angel heard, and straight appear'd,
        Mistaking earth for heav'n.

GRAND CHORUS

As from the pow'r of sacred lays   55
    The spheres began to move,
And sung the great Creator's praise
    To all the blest above;
So, when the last and dreadful hour
This crumbling pageant shall devour,   60
The Trumpet shall be heard on high,
The dead shall live, the living die,
And Music shall untune the sky.

Epilogue to King Arthur

SPOKEN BY MRS BRACEGIRDLE

I'VE had to-day a dozen *billets-doux*
From fops, and wits, and cits, and Bow Street *beaux;*
Some from Whitehall, but from the Temple more:
A Covent Garden porter brought me four.
I have not yet read all; but, without feigning,   5
We maids can make shrewd guesses at your meaning.
What if, to shew your styles, I read 'em here?
Methinks I hear one cry: "O Lord, forbear!
No, madam, no; by Heav'n, that's too severe."
Well then, be safe —   10
But swear henceforwards to renounce all writing,
And take this solemn oath of my inditing,
As you love ease, and hate campaigns and fighting.
Yet, faith, 't is just to make some few examples:
What if I shew'd you one or two for samples?   15
(*Pulls one out.*) Here 's one desires my ladyship to meet
At the kind couch above in Bridges Street.
O sharping knave! that would have you know what,
For a poor sneaking treat of chocolate.
(*Pulls out another.*) Now, in the name of luck, I 'll break this
     open,   20
Because I dreamt last night I had a token:
The superscription is exceeding pretty:
To the desire of all the town and city.
Now, gallants, you must know, this precious fop
Is foreman of a haberdasher's shop: 25
One who devoutly cheats, demure in carriage,
And courts me to the holy bands of marriage;
But with a civil innuendo too,
My overplus of love shall be for you.

(*Reads.*) "Madam, I swear your looks are so divine,   30
When I set up, your face shall be my sign:
Tho' times are hard, to shew how I adore you,
Here's my whole heart, and half a guinea for you.
But have a care of *beaux*; they 're false, my honey;
And, which is worse, have not one rag of money."   35
    See how maliciously the rogue would wrong ye!
But I know better things of some among ye.
My wisest way will be to keep the stage,
And trust to the good nature of the age;
And he that likes the music and the play   40
Shall be my favourite gallant to-day.

Song from King Arthur

SUNG BY VENUS IN HONOUR OF BRITANNIA

I

FAIREST isle, all isles excelling,
    Seat of pleasures and of loves;
Venus here will choose her dwelling,
    And forsake her Cyprian groves.

II

Cupid from his fav'rite nation   5
    Care and envy will remove;
Jealousy, that poisons passion,
    And despair, that dies for love.

III

Gentle murmurs, sweet complaining,
    Sighs that blow the fire of love;   10
Soft repulses, kind disdaining,
    Shall be all the pains you prove.

Every swain shall pay his duty,
  Grateful every nymph shall prove;
And as these excel in beauty,   15
  Those shall be renown'd for love.

The Lady's Song

I

A CHOIR of bright beauties in spring did appear,
To choose a May-lady to govern the year;
All the nymphs were in white, and the shepherds in green;
The garland was giv'n, and Phyllis was queen:
But Phyllis refus'd it, and sighing did say: 5
"I'll not wear a garland while Pan is away."

II

While Pan and fair Syrinx are fled from our shore,
The Graces are banish'd, and Love is no more:
The soft god of pleasure, that warm'd our desires,
Has broken his bow, and extinguish'd his fires;   10
And vows that himself and his mother will mourn,
Till Pan and fair Syrinx in triumph return.

III

Forbear your addresses, and court us no more,
For we will perform what the deity swore;
But if you dare think of deserving our charms,   15
Away with your sheephooks, and take to your arms:
Then laurels and myrtles your brows shall adorn,
When Pan, and his son, and fair Syrinx return.

Epilogue to Henry the Second, King of England with the Death of Rosamond

SPOKEN BY MRS BRACEGIRDLE

THUS you the sad catastrophe have seen,
  Occasion'd by a mistress and a queen.
  Queen Eleanor the proud was French, they say;
  But English manufacture got the day.
  Jane Clifford was her name, as books aver; 5
  Fair Rosamond was but her *nom de guerre*.
  Now tell me, gallants, would you lead your life
  With such a mistress, or with such a wife?
  If one must be your choice, which d'ye approve,
  The curtain lecture, or the curtain love? 10
  Would ye be godly with perpetual strife,
  Still drudging on with homely Joan your wife,
  Or take your pleasure in a wicked way,
  Like honest whoring Harry in the play?
  I guess your minds: the mistress would be taking, 15
  And nauseous matrimony sent a packing.
  The devil 's in ye all; mankind 's a rogue;
  You love the bride, but you detest the clog.
  After a year, poor spouse is left i' th' lurch,
  And you, like Haynes, return to Mother Church. 20
  Or, if the name of Church comes cross your mind,
  Chapels of ease behind our scenes you find.
  The playhouse is a kind of market place;
  One chaffers for a voice, another for a face:
  Nay, some of you, I dare not say how many, 25
  Would buy of me a pen'worth for your penny.
  Ev'n this poor face, which with my fan I hide,

Would make a shift my portion to provide,
With some small perquisites I have beside.
Tho' for your love, perhaps, I should not care,   30
I could not hate a man that bids me fair.
What might ensue, 't is hard for me to tell;
But I was drench'd to-day for loving well,
And fear the poison that would make me swell.

Song to a Fair Young Lady

GOING OUT OF THE TOWN IN THE SPRING

I

Ask not the cause, why sullen Spring
    So long delays her flow'rs to bear;
Why warbling birds forget to sing,
    And winter storms invert the year.
Chloris is gone, and fate provides   5
To make it spring where she resides.

II

Chloris is gone, the cruel fair:
    She cast not back a pitying eye;
But left her lover in despair,
    To sigh, to languish, and to die.   10
Ah, how can those fair eyes endure
To give the wounds they will not cure!

III

Great God of Love, why hast thou made
    A face that can all hearts command,
That all religions can invade,   15
    And change the laws of ev'ry land?
Where thou hadst plac'd such pow'r before,
Thou shouldst have made her mercy more.

When Chloris to the temple comes,
   Adoring crowds before her fall:
She can restore the dead from tombs,   20
   And ev'ry life but mine recall.
I only am by Love design'd
To be the victim for mankind.

To My Dear Friend Mr Congreve

on His Comedy call'd The Double-Dealer

WELL then, the promis'd hour is come at last;
The present age of wit obscures the past:
Strong were our sires, and as they fought they writ,
Conqu'ring with force of arms, and dint of wit;
Theirs was the giant race, before the flood;   5
And thus, when Charles return'd, our empire stood.
Like Janus he the stubborn soil manur'd,
With rules of husbandry the rankness cur'd;
Tam'd us to manners, when the stage was rude;
And boist'rous English wit with art indued.   10
Our age was cultivated thus at length,
But what we gain'd in skill we lost in strength.
Our builders were with want of genius curst;
The second temple was not like the first:
Till you, the best Vitruvius, come at length;   15
Our beauties equal, but excel our strength.
Firm Doric pillars found your solid base;
The fair Corinthian crowns the higher space:
Thus all below is strength, and all above is grace.
In easy dialogue is Fletcher's praise;   20
He mov'd the mind, but had not power to raise.

Great Jonson did by strength of judgment please;
Yet, doubling Fletcher's force, he wants his ease.
In differing talents both adorn'd their age;
One for the study, t'other for the stage: 25
But both to Congreve justly shall submit,
One match'd in judgment, both o'ermatch'd in wit.
In him all beauties of this age we see,
Etherege his courtship, Southerne's purity,
The satire, wit, and strength of Manly Wycherley.   30
All this in blooming youth you have achiev'd,
Nor are your foil'd contemporaries griev'd.
So much the sweetness of your manners move,
We cannot envy you, because we love.
Fabius might joy in Scipio, when he saw   35
A beardless consul made against the law;
And join his suffrage to the votes of Rome,
Tho' he with Hannibal was overcome.
Thus old Romano bow'd to Raphael's fame,
And scholar to the youth he taught became.   40

  O that your brows my laurel had sustain'd;
Well had I been depos'd, if you had reign'd!
The father had descended for the son;
For only you are lineal to the throne.
Thus, when the state one Edward did depose,   45
A greater Edward in his room arose.
But now, not I, but poetry is curst;
For Tom the Second reigns like Tom the First.
But let 'em not mistake my patron's part,
Nor call his charity their own desert.   50
Yet this I prophesy: thou shalt be seen
(Tho' with some short parenthesis between)
High on the throne of wit; and, seated there,
Not mine — that's little — but thy laurel wear.
Thy first attempt an early promise made;   55
That early promise this has more than paid.

So bold, yet so judiciously you dare,
That your least praise is to be regular.
Time, place, and action, may with pains be wrought;
But genius must be born, and never can be taught. 60
This is your portion; this your native store;
Heav'n, that but once was prodigal before,
To Shakespeare gave as much; she could not give him more.
   Maintain your post: that's all the fame you need;
For 't is impossible you should proceed. 65
Already I am worn with cares and age,
And just abandoning th' ungrateful stage;
Unprofitably kept at Heav'n's expense,
I live a rent-charge on his providence:
But you, whom ev'ry Muse and Grace adorn, 70
Whom I foresee to better fortune born,
Be kind to my remains; and O defend,
Against your judgment, your departed friend!
Let not the insulting foe my fame pursue,
But shade those laurels which descend to you; 75
And take for tribute what these lines express:
You merit more; nor could my love do less.

Extract from

The Aeneid of Virgil

Book Four

THE rosy morn was risen from the main,
And horns and hounds awake the princely train:
They issue early thro' the city gate,
Where the more wakeful huntsmen ready wait, 185
With nets, and toils, and darts, beside the force
Of Spartan dogs, and swift Massylian horse.

The Tyrian peers and officers of state
For the slow queen in antechambers wait;
Her lofty courser, in the court below,   190
Who his majestic rider seems to know,
Proud of his purple trappings, paws the ground,
And champs the golden bit, and spreads the foam around.
The queen at length appears; on either hand
The brawny guards in martial order stand.   195
A flow'r'd simar with golden fringe she wore,
And at her back a golden quiver bore;
Her flowing hair a golden caul restrains,
A golden clasp the Tyrian robe sustains.
Then young Ascanius, with a sprightly grace,   200
Leads on the Trojan youth to view the chase.
But far above the rest in beauty shines
The great Aeneas, when the troop he joins;
Like fair Apollo, when he leaves the frost
Of wint'ry Xanthus, and the Lycian coast,   205
When to his native Delos he resorts,
Ordains the dances, and renews the sports;
Where painted Scythians, mix'd with Cretan bands,
Before the joyful altars join their hands:
Himself, on Cynthus walking, sees below   210
The merry madness of the sacred show.
Green wreaths of bays his length of hair inclose;
A golden fillet binds his awful brows;
His quiver sounds: not less the prince is seen
In manly presence, or in lofty mien.   215
    Now had they reach'd the hills, and storm'd the seat
Of salvage beasts, in dens, their last retreat.
The cry pursues the mountain goats: they bound
From rock to rock, and keep the craggy ground;
Quite otherwise the stags, a trembling train,   220
In herds unsingled, scour the dusty plain,
And a long chase in open view maintain.

117

The glad Ascanius, as his courser guides,
Spurs thro' the vale, and these and those outrides.
His horse's flanks and sides are forc'd to feel   225
The clanking lash, and goring of the steel.
Impatiently he views the feeble prey,
Wishing some nobler beast to cross his way,
And rather would the tusky boar attend,
Or see the tawny lion downward bend.   230

    Meantime, the gath'ring clouds obscure the skies:
From pole to pole the forky lightning flies;
The rattling thunders roll; and Juno pours
A wintry deluge down, and sounding show'rs.
The company, dispers'd, to coverts ride,   235
And seek the homely cots, or mountain's hollow side.
The rapid rains, descending from the hills,
To rolling torrents raise the creeping rills.
The queen and prince, as love or fortune guides,
One common cavern in her bosom hides.   240
Then first the trembling earth the signal gave,
And flashing fires enlighten all the cave;
Hell from below, and Juno from above,
And howling nymphs, were conscious to their love.
From this ill-omen'd hour in time arose   245
Debate and death, and all succeeding woes.

To My Honour'd Kinsman, John Driden,

of Chesterton, in the County of Huntingdon, Esquire

How blest is he, who leads a country life,
Unvex'd with anxious cares, and void of strife!
Who, studying peace and shunning civil rage,
Enjoy'd his youth, and now enjoys his age:

All who deserve his love, he makes his own;   5
And, to be lov'd himself, needs only to be known.

Just, good, and wise, contending neighbours come,
From your award to wait their final doom;
And, foes before, return in friendship home.
Without their cost, you terminate the cause,   10
And save th' expense of long litigious laws:
Where suits are travers'd, and so little won,
That he who conquers is but last undone.
Such are not your decrees; but so design'd,
The sanction leaves a lasting peace behind: 15
Like your own soul, serene; a pattern of your mind.

Promoting concord, and composing strife,
Lord of yourself, uncumber'd with a wife;
Where, for a year, a month, perhaps a night,
Long penitence succeeds a short delight: 20
Minds are so hardly match'd, that ev'n the first,
Tho' pair'd by Heav'n, in Paradise were curst.
For man and woman, tho' in one they grow,
Yet, first or last, return again to two.
He to God's image, she to his was made;   25
So, farther from the fount, the stream at random stray'd.

How could he stand, when, put to double pain,
He must a weaker than himself sustain!
Each might have stood perhaps, but each alone;
Two wrestlers help to pull each other down.   30

Not that my verse would blemish all the fair;
But yet if *some* be bad, 't is wisdom to beware;
And better shun the bait than struggle in the snare.
Thus have you shunn'd, and shun, the married state,
Trusting as little as you can to fate.   35

No porter guards the passage of your door,
T' admit the wealthy, and exclude the poor;
For God, who gave the riches, gave the heart,
To sanctify the whole, by giving part.

Heav'n, who foresaw the will, the means has wrought, 40
And to the second son a blessing brought;
The first-begotten had his father's share,
But you, like Jacob, are Rebecca's heir.

So may your stores and fruitful fields increase;
And ever be you blest, who live to bless. 45
As Ceres sow'd, where'er her chariot flew;
As Heav'n in desarts rain'd the bread of dew;
So free to many, to relations most,
You feed with manna your own Israel host.

With crowds attended of your ancient race, 50
You seek the champian sports or sylvan chase;
With well-breath'd beagles you surround the wood,
Ev'n then industrious of the common good;
And often have you brought the wily fox
To suffer for the firstlings of the flocks; 55
Chas'd ev'n amid the folds, and made to bleed,
Like felons, where they did the murd'rous deed.
This fiery game your active youth maintain'd,
Not yet by years extinguish'd, tho' restrain'd:
You season still with sports your serious hours; 60
For age but tastes of pleasures, youth devours.
The hare in pastures or in plains is found,
Emblem of human life, who runs the round;
And after all his wand'ring ways are done,
His circle fills and ends where he begun, 65
Just as the setting meets the rising sun.

Thus princes ease their cares; but happier he
Who seeks not pleasure thro' necessity,
Than such as once on slipp'ry thrones were plac'd,
And chasing, sigh to think themselves are chas'd. 70

So liv'd our sires, ere doctors learn'd to kill,
And multiplied with theirs the weekly bill.
The first physicians by debauch were made;
Excess began, and sloth sustains the trade.

Pity the gen'rous kind their cares bestow   75
To search forbidden truths; (a sin to know:)
To which if human science could attain,
The doom of death, pronounc'd by God, were vain.
In vain the leech would interpose delay;
Fate fastens first, and vindicates the prey.   80
What help from art's endeavours can we have?
Gibbons but guesses, nor is sure to save;
But Maurus sweeps whole parishes, and peoples ev'ry grave;
And no more mercy to mankind will use,
Than when he robb'd and murder'd Maro's Muse.   85
Wouldst thou be soon dispatch'd, and perish whole?
Trust Maurus with thy life, and M—lb—rne with thy soul.

By chase our long-liv'd fathers earn'd their food;
Toil strung the nerves and purified the blood:
But we, their sons, a pamper'd race of men,   90
Are dwindled down to threescore years and ten.
Better to hunt in fields for health unbought
Than fee the doctor for a nauseous draught.
The wise for cure on exercise depend;
God never made his work for man to mend.   95
The tree of knowledge, once in Eden plac'd,
Was easy found, but was forbid the taste:
O had our grandsire walk'd without his wife,
He first had sought the better plant of life!
Now, both are lost; yet, wand'ring in the dark,   100
Physicians, for the tree, have found the bark.
They, lab'ring for relief of humankind,
With sharpen'd sight some remedies may find;
Th' apothecary train is wholly blind.
From files a random recipe they take,   105
And many deaths of one prescription make.
Garth, gen'rous as his Muse, prescribes and gives;
The shopman sells, and by destruction lives:
Ungrateful tribe! who, like the viper's brood,

From med'cine issuing, suck their mother's blood! 110
Let these obey, and let the learn'd prescribe,
That men may die without a double bribe:
Let them but under their superiors kill,
When doctors first have sign'd the bloody bill;
He scapes the best, who, nature to repair, 115
Draws physic from the fields, in draughts of vital air.

You hoard not health for your own private use,
But on the public spend the rich produce;
When, often urg'd, unwilling to be great,
Your country calls you from your lov'd retreat, 120
And sends to senates, charg'd with common care,
Which none more shuns, and none can better bear.
Where could they find another form'd so fit,
To poise with solid sense a sprightly wit?
Were these both wanting, (as they both abound,) 125
Where could so firm integrity be found?

Well-born, and wealthy, wanting no support,
You steer betwixt the country and the court;
Nor gratify whate'er the great desire,
Nor grudging give what public needs require. 130
Part must be left, a fund when foes invade;
And part employ'd to roll the wat'ry trade:
Ev'n Canaan's happy land, when worn with toil,
Requir'd a sabbath year to mend the meagre soil.

Good senators (and such are you) so give, 135
That kings may be supplied, the people thrive.
And he, when want requires, is truly wise,
Who slights not foreign aids, nor over-buys,
But on our native strength, in time of need, relies.
Munster was bought, we boast not the success; 140
Who fights for gain, for greater makes his peace.

Our foes, compell'd by need, have peace embrac'd;
The peace both parties want is like to last:
Which if secure, securely we may trade;

Or, not secure, should never have been made.   145
Safe in ourselves, while on ourselves we stand,
The sea is ours, and that defends the land.
Be, then, the naval stores the nation's care,
New ships to build, and batter'd to repair.

  Observe the war, in ev'ry annual course;   150
What has been done was done with British force:
Namur subdued is England's palm alone;
The rest besieg'd, but we constrain'd the town:
We saw th' event that follow'd our success;
France, tho' pretending arms, pursued the peace;   155
Oblig'd, by one sole treaty, to restore
What twenty years of war had won before.
Enough for Europe has our Albion fought:
Let us enjoy the peace our blood has bought.
When once the Persian king was put to flight.   160
The weary Macedons refus'd to fight,
Themselves their own mortality confess'd,
And left the son of Jove to quarrel for the rest.

  Ev'n victors are by victories undone;
Thus Hannibal, with foreign laurels won,   165
To Carthage was recall'd, too late to keep his own.
While sore of battle, while our wounds are green,
Why should we tempt the doubtful die again?
In wars renew'd, uncertain of success;
Sure of a share, as umpires of the peace.   170

  A patriot both the king and country serves;
Prerogative and privilege preserves:
Of each our laws the certain limit show;
One must not ebb, nor t'other overflow.
Betwixt the prince and parliament we stand;   175
The barriers of the state on either hand:
May neither overflow, for then they drown the land!
When both are full, they feed our blest abode;
Like those that water'd once the paradise of God.

Some overpoise of sway by turns they share;   180
In peace the people, and the prince in war:
Consuls of mod'rate pow'r in calms were made;
When the Gauls came, one sole dictator sway'd.
    Patriots, in peace, assert the people's right;
With noble stubbornness resisting might: 185
No lawless mandates from the court receive,
Nor lend by force, but in a body give.
Such was your gen'rous grandsire; free to grant
In parliaments that weigh'd their prince's want:
But so tenacious of the common cause,   190
As not to lend the king against his laws;
And, in a loathsome dungeon doom'd to lie,
In bonds retain'd his birthright liberty,
And sham'd oppression, till it set him free.
    O true descendant of a patriot line,   195
Who, while thou shar'st their lustre, lend'st 'em thine,
Vouchsafe this picture of thy soul to see;
'T is so far good, as it resembles thee.
The beauties to th' original I owe;
Which when I miss, my own defects I show: 200
Nor think the kindred Muses thy disgrace;
A poet is not born in ev'ry race.
Two of a house few ages can afford;
One to perform, another to record.
Praiseworthy actions are by thee embrac'd;   205
And 't is my praise, to make thy praises last.
For ev'n when death dissolves our human frame,
The soul returns to heav'n, from whence it came;
Earth keeps the body, verse preserves the fame.

The Cock and the Fox

OR, THE TALE OF THE NUN'S PRIEST

FROM CHAUCER

THERE liv'd, as authors tell, in days of yore,
A widow somewhat old, and very poor:
Deep in a dell her cottage lonely stood,
Well thatch'd, and under covert of a wood.
   This dowager, on whom my tale I found,   5
Since last she laid her husband in the ground,
A simple sober life in patience led,
And had but just enough to buy her bread:
But huswifing the little Heav'n had lent,
She duly paid a groat for quarter rent;   10
And pinch'd her belly, with her daughters two,
To bring the year about with much ado.
   The cattle in her homestead were three sows,
An ewe call'd Mally, and three brinded cows;
Her parlour window stuck with herbs around,   15
Of sav'ry smell; and rushes strew'd the ground.
A maple dresser in her hall she had,
On which full many a slender meal she made:
For no delicious morsel pass'd her throat;
According to her cloth she cut her coat.   20
No poynant sauce she knew, no costly treat;
Her hunger gave a relish to her meat;
A sparing diet did her health assure;
Or sick, a pepper posset was her cure.
Before the day was done, her work she sped,   25
And never went by candlelight to bed.
With exercise she sweat ill humours out;

Her dancing was not hinder'd by the gout.
Her poverty was glad, her heart content,
Nor knew she what the spleen or vapours meant. 30
Of wine she never tasted thro' the year,
But white and black was all her homely cheer:
Brown bread, and milk, (but first she skimm'd her bowls,)
And rashers of sing'd bacon on the coals.
On holidays an egg, or two at most; 35
But her ambition never reach'd to roast.

The Secular Masque

Enter JANUS]

JANUS

Chronos, Chronos, mend thy pace;
  An hundred times the rolling sun
  Around the radiant belt has run
In his revolving race.
Behold, behold, the goal in sight; 5
Spread thy fans, and wing thy flight.

Enter CHRONOS, *with a scythe in his hand, and a great
globe on his back, which he sets down at his entrance.*]

CHRONOS

Weary, weary of my weight,
Let me, let me drop my freight,
  And leave the world behind.
I could not bear 10
Another year
  The load of humankind.

Enter MOMUS, *laughing*]

MOMUS

Ha! ha! ha! ha! ha! ha! well hast thou done
  To lay down thy pack,
  And lighten thy back;   15
The world was a fool, e'er since it begun,
And since neither Janus, nor Chronos, nor I
  Can hinder the crimes,
  Or mend the bad times,
'T is better to laugh than to cry.   20

CHORUS *of all Three*
'T is better to laugh than to cry.

JANUS

Since Momus comes to laugh below,
  Old Time, begin the show,
That he may see, in every scene,
What changes in this age have been.   25

CHRONOS

Then, goddess of the silver bow, begin.
Horns, or hunting music within.]

Enter DIANA]

DIANA

With horns and with hounds I waken the day,
And hie to my woodland walks away;
I tuck up my robe, and am buskin'd soon,
And tie to my forehead a wexing moon.   30
I course the fleet stag, unkennel the fox,
And chase the wild goats o'er summits of rocks;
With shouting and hooting we pierce thro' the sky,
And Echo turns hunter, and doubles the cry.

CHORUS of All
With shouting and hooting we pierce thro' the sky,
And Echo turns hunter, and doubles the cry.

JANUS
Then our age was in its prime:

CHRONOS
Free from rage:

DIANA
And free from crime:

MOMUS
A very merry, dancing, drinking,
Laughing, quaffing, and unthinking time.

CHORUS of All
Then our age was in its prime,
Free from rage, and free from crime;
A very merry, dancing, drinking,
Laughing, quaffing, and unthinking time.

Dance of DIANA's *attendants.*]

Enter MARS]

MARS
Inspire the vocal brass, inspire;
The world is past its infant age:
   Arms and honour,
   Arms and honour,
Set the martial mind on fire,
And kindle manly rage.
Mars has look'd the sky to red;
And Peace, the lazy good, is fled.
Plenty, Peace, and Pleasure fly;

The sprightly green
In woodland walks no more is seen; 55
The sprightly green has drunk the Tyrian dye.

CHORUS *of All*
Plenty, Peace, &c.

MARS
Sound the trumpet, beat the drum;
   Thro' all the world around,
   Sound a reveille, sound, sound, 60
The warrior god is come.

CHORUS *of All*
Sound the trumpet, &c.

MOMUS
Thy sword within the scabbard keep,
   And let mankind agree;
Better the world were fast asleep, 65
   Than kept awake by thee.
The fools are only thinner,
   With all our cost and care;
But neither side a winner,
   For things are as they were. 70

CHORUS *of All*
The fools are only, &c.

Enter VENUS]

VENUS
Calms appear when storms are past,
Love will have his hour at last:
Nature is my kindly care;
Mars destroys, and I repair; 75
Take me, take me, while you may;
Venus comes not ev'ry day.

CHORUS *of All*

Take her, take her, &c.

CHRONOS

The world was then so light,
I scarcely felt the weight;   80
Joy rul'd the day, and Love the night.
But since the Queen of Pleasure left the ground,
  I faint, I lag,
  And feebly drag
The pond'rous orb around.   85

MOMUS

All, all of a piece throughout:
Pointing to DIANA.]
  Thy chase had a beast in view;
To MARS]
  Thy wars brought nothing about;
To VENUS]
  Thy lovers were all untrue.

JANUS

'T is well an old age is out: 90

CHRONOS

And time to begin a new.

CHORUS *of All*

All, all of a piece throughout:
Thy chase had a beast in view;
Thy wars brought nothing about;
Thy lovers were all untrue.   95
'T is well an old age is out,
And time to begin a new.

Dance of huntsmen, nymphs, warriors, and lovers.]

130

COMMENTARY AND NOTES

27. TO MY HONOUR'D FRIEND, DR CHARLETON

In this poem Dryden shows his interest in the new scientific ideas of the time and their challenge to ancient authority. Charleton had sponsored his entry into the Royal Society and written a book, in opposition to the views of Inigo Jones, to show that Stonehenge had been a Danish palace (*Chorea Gigantum*, 1663). Dryden's poem first appeared in this book.

3. *the Stagirite:* Aristotle, who was born at Stagira.

25. *Gilbert:* William Gilbert (1540–1603), founder of the science of magnetism and author of *De Magnete* (1600).

27. *Boyle:* Robert Boyle (1627–91), experimental chemist and theologian, brother of the Earl of Orrery, statesman and poet.

31. *Harvey:* William Harvey (1578–1657), discoverer of the circulation of the blood.

32. *Ent:* Sir George Ent (1604–89), an original Fellow of the Royal Society, who had defended Harvey.

53–4. Charles II is said to have visited Stonehenge after his defeat at Worcester (1651).

29. *Extract from* ANNUS MIRABILIS: THE YEAR OF WONDERS, 1666

London had just endured the Great Plague of 1665 and this was followed in September 1666 by the Great Fire which destroyed much of the old city. In the course of the summer there had been many severe naval actions with the Dutch in which the English fleets had had varying success. There had been prophecies of disaster and judgment upon the nation, and Dryden wrote his poem to stress the heroic aspect of the Dutch War, the commercial vigour of the country, and the technical skill and enterprise of its people. In method it is a highly experimental poem, not less so because it makes use of specialist terms and a technological vocabulary in the manner of Virgil's *Georgics*; the heroic mode is adapted to an immediate, contemporary theme, the glorification of empirical, scientific-minded Restoration England.

The quatrain with alternate rhymes had been used by Sir William Davenant in his heroic poem *Gondibert* (1651), and Dryden considered it at this stage of his career as eminently suitable for heroic verse, 'more noble and of greater dignity' than other metres. It is uncommonly slow for narrative (it is perhaps more familiar as the metre of Gray's *Elegy*). The stanzas given, the last in the poem, foretell how a new London will rise from the ruins of the old.

1169. *chymic:* alchemic, turning to gold.

1171. *the town which gives the Indies name:* 'Mexico' (Dryden's note).

1173. Wren had laid a plan for the rebuilding of London before the King and council as early as 10 September.

1177. *more August:* 'Augusta, the old name of London' (Dryden's note).

31. *Epilogue to* TYRANNICK LOVE

Prologues and epilogues in verse, often quite unrelated to the content of the play, were used on the English stage from the time of Shakespeare until late in the eighteenth century. After the Restoration they were aimed at establishing a bond with the small, highly sophisticated London audience. Dryden is a master of the colloquial casualness necessary for the success of the form; his services were greatly in demand by other dramatists, and he is said to have made as much as six guineas by a prologue, at a time when the total profits of a playwright (from the third night's performance) might come as low as twenty pounds.

Tyrannick Love was first performed in 1669, about the time Nell Gwyn became Charles II's mistress. ('Mrs Ellen' is Nell Gwyn.)

the bearers: the stage hands.

13. *taking:* being put under a spell or enchantment.

25. *make haste to me:* i.e. in hell.

30. *Cathar'n:* colloquially pronounced to rhyme with 'slattern'.

32. *Epilogue to the Second Part of* THE CONQUEST OF GRANADA

Dryden here expounds his belief in the greater linguistic refinement of his own age over that of Shakespeare and Jonson. He develops the argument in a prose essay, *A Defence of the Epilogue*, printed with the early editions of the play. There he says: 'It is . . . my part to make it clear, that the Language, Wit, and Conversation of our Age are improv'd and refin'd above the last; and then it will not be difficult to inferr, that our Playes have receiv'd some part of those advantages'.

6. *Cob's tankard . . . Otter's horse:* characters in Jonson's *Every Man in his Humour* and *The Silent Woman* respectively. Each jests about his tankard, and the latter calls his his horse.

33. *Song from* MARRIAGE À LA MODE

Sung by Doralice and Beliza. The play was probably first performed in 1672.

3. *following nature:* studying reality in a scientific manner, which is opposed in the next line to 'wit' or cultivating the imagination.

13. *the little world:* the nature of man, thought of in the old cosmology as a microcosm, or model in little, of the universe (the macrocosm, or great world).

14. *the sphere of crystal:* Merlin's sphere of crystal is described in *The Faerie Queene*, III. ii. 19:

> It vertue had, to shew in perfect sight,
> What euer thing was in the world contaynd,
> Betwixt the lowest earth and heauens hight,
> So that it to the looker appertaynd.

27. *see th' offended God, and die:* Exod. xx. 19.

35. Prologue to AURENG-ZEBE

37. *our neighbours:* the other theatre company, the Duke's at Dorset Garden; Dryden wrote for the King's company.

37. Song from THE SPANISH FRIAR

The play was first performed in 1680.

38. ABSALOM AND ACHITOPHEL, PART ONE

The Whig party under their leader the Earl of Shaftesbury opposed the succession of Charles II's brother, James, Duke of York, since he was a Roman Catholic; they supported the claim of James, Duke of Monmouth, Charles's son by Lucy Walter. A bill to exclude the Duke of York from the throne passed the House of Commons, but in 1681 the tide turned. Charles dissolved his Parliament at Oxford and made a successful appeal to the country; Shaftesbury was arrested and put in the Tower, and Monmouth was later placed under restraint.

Dryden's poem, said to have been undertaken at the King's request, was a move in the later stages of the Tory counter-attack; but in the skill with which it dramatizes the central figures, and in the poet's unprejudiced eye for character, it rises above politics into literature. In doing so it makes a perennial statement about the nature of power and the behaviour of a political community at a time of crisis.

The biblical parallel was not new. Others had made use of it to satirize or defend both Charles II and his father (see R. F. Jones, 'The Originality

of *Absalom and Achitophel*', *Modern Language Notes*, xlvi. (1931) 211–18).
The key to the principal figures in the allegory is as follows:

David	Charles
Absalom	the Duke of Monmouth
Achitophel	Anthony Ashley Cooper, Earl of Shaftesbury
Zimri	the Duke of Buckingham
the Jews	the English
Jebusites	Roman Catholics
Israel	England
Sion or Jerusalem	London
Hebron	Scotland
Jordan	the Channel

The first complete key to the poem was printed by Tonson in *The First Part of the Miscellany Poems* in 1716.

7. *Israel's monarch, after heaven's own heart*: cf. 1 Sam. xiii. 13–14.

11. *Michal*: Catherine of Braganza, Princess of Portugal (1638–1705), who was married to Charles II in 1662.

18. *Absalom*: James Scott (1649–85), Charles's illegitimate son by Lucy Walter, who had been created Duke of Monmouth in 1663; he won a reputation as a soldier, and possessed courage and great personal charm. Though banished to Holland for his intrigues against the Duke of York, he returned and began a quasi-royal progress through the western counties; he was subsequently involved in the Rye House Plot, but pardoned, and again banished from the court. On James II's accession he led the luckless rebellion in the west which ended in defeat at Sedgemoor and his own death on the scaffold.

20. *gust*: pleasure or satisfaction.

34. *Annabel*: Monmouth's wife, Anne, Countess of Buccleuch (1651–1732).

39. *Amnon's murther*: probably refers to the slitting of Sir John Coventry's nose at Monmouth's instigation in 1670. Cf. 2 Sam. xiii. See James Kinsley, 'Historical Allusions in *Absalom and Achitophel*', *Review of English Studies*, N.S. vi. (1955) 291–7.

44. *proves*: tests.

51. *Adam-wits*: i.e. they were like Adam, who wanted the fruit of the tree of knowledge though granted all else in Eden.

55. *woods and caves*: the places where the Nonconformists held their conventicles; but Sir Charles Firth sees an allusion to the Hobbesian state of nature.

57–8. *Saul . . . Ishbosheth*: Oliver Cromwell and his son Richard.

99. *Hebron:* the young Charles II was crowned in Scotland on 1 January 1651.

66. *a state:* a republic.

82. *the Good Old Cause:* the cause of the Puritan Commonwealth.

108. *that plot:* the Popish Plot; the false information given by Titus Oates and others led to the arrest and execution of many prominent Catholics. 'The Witnesses led the Rabble; the Plot-Managers led the Witnesses; and the Devil himself led the Leaders.' (Roger L'Estrange, *A Brief History*, 1687.)

118. *Egyptian rites:* Egypt is Catholic France.

120–1. A sneer at the doctrine of transubstantiation.

129. *the fleece:* the tithes paid to the Anglican clergy by their parishioners.

144. *thrown:* like the angels cast down with Lucifer from heaven; anticipating the 'fiends' of the next line.

150. *the false Achitophel:* Anthony Ashley Cooper (1621–83) fought on both sides in the Civil War and was a member of Cromwell's Parliaments and of his Council of State. He promoted the Restoration, was created Earl of Shaftesbury in 1672, and became Lord Chancellor. He was the principal leader of the Whig opposition. 'He had a wonderful faculty at opposing, and running things down; but had not the like force in building up.' (Burnet, *History of His Own Time* (1724–34) i. 96.)

157. *Fretted:* wore out, consumed.

158. *o'er informed:* filled the vessel of the body beyond its capacity; over-charged it.

170–1. *that unfeather'd, two legg'd thing:* Plato is said thus to have defined man, Diogenes Laertius, vi. 40.

175. *the triple bond:* the Triple Alliance of England, Holland, and Sweden. Shaftesbury and the Cabal broke it by negotiating with Louis XIV and bringing on the Third Dutch War of 1672–4.

188. *Abbethdin:* the judge of a Jewish court (literally 'father of the court of justice') alluding to Shaftesbury's service as Lord Chancellor.

197. David would have sung Achitophel's praises instead of composing one of his Psalms; there is perhaps a reference to Charles II's speech to his Oxford Parliament or to the successful appeal to the country he later published (*His Majesties Declaration to all His Loving Subjects*, 1681). The point would then be that if Shaftesbury had remained loyal this declaration would have been unnecessary, or might indeed have spoken in Shaftesbury's favour.

204. *manifest of:* evidently guilty of (Latin, *manifestus sceleris*).

213. *a Jebusite:* Charles II declared himself a Catholic on his deathbed.

216. *the prime:* applied to the golden number, the number of any year in the lunar cycle of nineteen years. About this amount of time elapsed between the Long Parliament and the Restoration, and again between the Restoration and the Popish Plot.

227. Dryden found this line in *Lachrymae Musarum* (1649), the volume to which he had contributed 'Upon the Death of the Lord Hastings', and liked it sufficiently to use it again in *The Hind and the Panther*, i. 211.

228. *Him he attempts:* The Miltonic inversion and the phrase 'studied arts' recall Satan's temptation of Eve.

239. Joel ii. 28.

242. *pomps:* an allusion to Monmouth's triumphal progress through the west; the word's semantic history connects it with the idea of a procession.

264. *Gath:* Brussels, where Charles spent his exile.

270. *Jordan's sand:* Dover beach, where he landed in 1660.

281. *Pharaoh:* Louis XIV.

302. *the mouldy rolls of Noah's ark:* ancient pedigrees; perhaps referring to the attempt to trace the Stuart line back to Adam in Sir Robert Filmer's *Patriarchia* (1680).

353. *his brother:* James, Duke of York.

373. Another echo of the temptation in Eden.

390. *Sanhedrin:* Parliament; the council of the Jews.

411. Dryden reproduces the then fashionable view of Hobbes.

418. The Commonwealth (1649–53) when England had no king, preceded the personal rule of Cromwell.

438. A reference to the Border estates of Monmouth's wife as Countess of Buccleuch.

513. *the Solymaean rout:* the London mob. Solyma was another name for Jerusalem.

517. *an ethnic plot:* the Popish Plot, made by the Gentiles (τὰ ἔθνη), Jebusites, or Catholics.

519. *Hot Levites:* the dissenting ministers ejected in 1662.

525. *Aaron's race:* the priesthood.

541. *Hydra:* a many-headed monster that sprouted new heads as they were cut off.

544. *Zimri:* George Villiers (1628–87), second Duke of Buckingham, was the King's chief adviser after the fall of Clarendon, but was impeached in 1674 and became a leader of the opposition. He had a reputation as a profligate and a dilettante. He had ridiculed Dryden under the name of 'John Bayes' in *The Rehearsal* (1671). Dryden's choice of name, that of the paramour of Cozbi the Midianite (Num. xxv.) may refer to the story that he had been the lover of the Countess of Shrewsbury and the slayer of her husband.

574. *well hung Balaam:* Theophilus Hastings, Earl of Huntingdon. Well hung can mean (i) fluent, or (ii) having large pendent testicles, potent.
cold Caleb: Arthur Capel, Earl of Essex.

575-6. *canting Nadab:* William, Lord Howard of Escrick. He is said while in the Tower to have received the sacrament in *lamb's wool*—ale poured on roasted apples and sugar. It was Nadab who 'offered strange fire before the Lord' (Lev. x. 1).

576. *porridge:* hotch-potch; Nonconformist slang for the Anglican service and prayer book.

581. *bull-fac'd Jonas:* Sir William Jones, Attorney-General, who prosecuted those brought to trial during the Plot.

585. *Shimei:* Slingsby Bethel, Whig sheriff of London, and notorious for a stinginess not usual in that office.

595. *vare:* staff of office.

598. *sons of Belial:* implies rebellion rather than immorality (Deut. xiii. 13); there may be a pun on Balliol, where the Whig leaders were lodged at the time of the Oxford Parliament.

617. *Rechabites:* abstainers from strong drink (Jer. xxxv. 14).

632. *Corah:* Titus Oates, the contriver of the Plot, whose perjured evidence brought many to the scaffold. At the time of the poem's publication his power was on the wane.

633. *monumental brass:* Oates is compared to the brazen serpent erected by Moses which preserved the children of Israel (Num. xxi. 6–9).

644. *a Levite:* Oates had been an Anglican clergyman.

646. Sarcastic: these were in fact the accepted physical signs of a choleric temperament.

649. I.e. like a ruddy-faced parson, but his face also shone with the prophetic illumination of Moses when he came down from Mount Sinai.

658–9. Oates had falsely claimed to be a doctor of the University of Salamanca.

674. Oates had accused the Queen of conspiring with her physician to murder the King.

676. *Agag's murder:* this was once thought to refer to the murder of Sir Edmund Berry Godfrey, the magistrate who received the first depositions concerning the Plot. But Agag is more likely to stand for Lord Stafford, a Catholic peer who was executed in 1680 as a result of Oates' perjured evidence. See James Kinsley, 'Historical Allusions in *Absalom and Achitophel*', *ut supra.*

688. *to show:* modern English, 'on show'.

697. *Hybla:* a town in ancient Sicily famous for its honey.

705. *Egypt and Tyrus:* France and Holland.

710. *Bathsheba:* Louise de Kéroualle, Duchess of Portsmouth, Charles II's last and favourite mistress, is given the name of David's paramour.

729. The reference is to Monmouth's progress through the western counties.

738. *Wise Issachar:* Thomas Thynne of Longleat, a landowner favourable to the Whigs. The biblical Issachar is described as 'a strong ass couching down between two burdens' (Gen. xlix. 14); Professor Kinsley has

suggested that Thynne's two burdens were the expense of entertaining Monmouth and the financial liabilities of Lady Ogle, his wife.

759–810. In these lines Dryden summarizes his political philosophy. He agrees with Hobbes that the people have made over their sovereignty to their kings or rulers by a contract in order to avoid anarchy; he does not, however, think with Hobbes that the contract is indissoluble, nor with the Whigs that it can be revoked by the people's will. He takes an empirical middle course: innovation for its own sake is dangerous; change may only be permitted in extreme cases to preserve good order. On Dryden's sceptical conservatism cf. Louis I. Bredvold, *The Intellectual Milieu of John Dryden* (Ann Arbor: 1956), pp. 145–50.

769–74. The social contract binds the descendants of primitive men just as Adam's disobedience makes all succeeding generations of mankind guilty of original sin. The argument from the Fall would have seemed quite relevant to political discussion in the seventeenth century.

786. The higher the tide, the more rapid is the fall of water at the ebb.

794. *nature's state:* the state of nature when men lived in savagery before the foundation of civil society (Hobbes, *Leviathan*, i. 13).

817. *Barzillai:* James Butler, Duke of Ormonde, Lord Lieutenant of Ireland. He had remained continuously loyal to Charles I and II.

825 *practis'd:* frequented. One of Dryden's many French turns of phrase.

831. *His eldest hope:* Ormonde's eldest son, Thomas, Earl of Ossory, a distinguished soldier and sailor, died in 1680.

844–5. Dryden paraphrases Virgil, *Aeneid*, vi. 878–80.

859. *hearse:* the structure erected over a bier to carry coats of arms and funeral tributes.

864. *Zadoc the priest:* William Sancroft, Archbishop of Canterbury.

866. *the Sagan of Jerusalem:* Henry Compton, Bishop of London. The Sagan was the Jewish high priest's deputy.

868. *him of the western dome:* John Dolben, Dean of Westminster.

870. *the prophet's sons:* the boys of Westminster School.

877. *Sharp-judging Adriel:* John Sheffield, Earl of Mulgrave, and later Marquis of Normanby. He was a poet as well as a courtier, and his *Essay upon Satire* was ascribed to Dryden.

882. *Jotham:* George Savile, Viscount and later Marquis of Halifax, a trusted adviser of Charles in the last years of his reign. He was a 'Trimmer', who tried to steer a moderate course between the two parties. Jotham protested against the usurper Abimelech (Judges ix. 1–21).

888. *Hushai:* Laurence Hyde, Earl of Rochester, First Lord of the Treasury.

899. *Amiel:* Edward Seymour, Speaker of the House of Commons.

910. *th' unequal ruler of the day:* Phaeton, who drove the horses of the day too near the sun.

920. *plume:* pluck, a term from hawking.

138

939–1025. Pope told Spence that in these lines Dryden had versified Charles's speech to his Oxford Parliament. There are many resemblances to the pamphlet *His Majesties Declaration*. See Godfrey Davies, *Huntington Library Quarterly*, x. (1946) 69–82.

944. *my forgiving right:* Charles had on several occasions attempted to pardon those condemned for treason or to mitigate their penalties.

987. *unsatiate as the barren womb or grave:* Prov. xxx. 15–16: 'four things say not, It is enough: the grave; and the barren womb; the earth that is not filled with water; and the fire'.

1007–8. *Grace, Her hinder parts:* the hinder parts of grace. Cf. the Lord to Moses on Mount Sinai: 'For there shall no man see me, and live' (Exod. xxxiii. 20–3).

1012. *Against themselves:* many of the professional informers who had given evidence against Catholics during the Plot were ready to betray their own leaders when the Exclusion party fell from power.

1013. *viper-like:* the viper was supposed to tear itself from its mother's womb.

1028–9. *a series of new time:* Dryden associates Charles's political victory with the renewal of the golden age prophesied in Virgil's Fourth Eclogue.

68. *Extract from* THE MEDAL

The subject is said to have been suggested to Dryden by Charles II. Shaftesbury had been charged with high treason, but the grand jury threw out the bill against him to the delight of the Whig-inclined London mob. His friends struck a medal in his honour bearing his bust, with on the reverse side a view of London and the Tower showing the sun breaking through a cloud and underneath the inscription 'Laetamur' ('let us rejoice').

Dryden is said to have been rewarded for the poem with 'a present of a hundred broad pieces'.

The satire deals much more bitterly with Shaftesbury than does *Absalom and Achitophel*. The passage given is a typical analysis of the folly of the mob.

94. *thy Pindaric way:* in an irregular and impassioned manner like the Pindaric odes of the time. The long line is irregular to suit the sense.

96. *Phocion . . . Socrates:* Socrates and Phocion were put to death by the Athenian democracy, the one for treason, the other for impiety; in each case the state repented of its decision.

100. *the father . . . the son:* Charles I and his son Charles II.

119. *Jehu:* 2 Kings ix. 20.

129. *our usurping brave:* Cromwell. 'Brave', a bully, a bravo.

131. *we long for quails:* as did the Israelites when fed by God with manna in the wilderness.

This spirited and vigorous poem is a lampoon, a humorous personal attack rather than a serious satire on the abuses of the age, like Pope's *Dunciad* or his *Imitations of Horace*. It was probably written in 1678 and circulated in manuscript. In 1682 a bookseller obtained a copy of it and it was published.

Thomas Shadwell (1642?–92) was a comic dramatist and a rival of Dryden. He claimed to follow Ben Jonson in the tradition of the comedy of humours, or eccentric types, while Dryden had assisted in the development of the new, polished comedy of manners which is the particular achievement of the Restoration. His plays contain broad dialogue and a good deal of knockabout farce which is referred to in the course of the poem. Shadwell had praised *The Rehearsal*—an attack on Dryden—in the dedication to his play *The History of Timon of Athens* (1678), and the superciliousness of his allusion to his rival seems to have introduced an element of personal animosity into what had been so far a critical debate between the two poets.

The sub-title, implying that Shadwell was a keen Whig in his attitude to church government, appears to have been added by the publisher.

Richard Flecknoe (who died in 1678), a notoriously bad minor poet and playwright, is chosen to represent the king of dullness or bad literature.

9. *business:* the word could mean in slang, sexual intercourse, so there is an innuendo here.

25. *goodly fabric:* Shadwell was a large corpulent man.

29. *Heywood and Shirley:* Thomas Heywood (*c.* 1574–1641) had a long and prolific career as a dramatist in the Elizabethan period. His rollicking domestic comedies make him a suitable figure for Dryden to associate with the cruder popular style he attributes to Shadwell. James Shirley (1596–1666), dramatist of the Caroline period, some of whose comedies of London life (e.g. *The City Madam*) anticipate the Restoration mode.

types: persons or incidents in the Old Testament foreshadowing others in the New.

32–4. A blasphemous allusion to the mission of St John the Baptist. *Norwich drugget:* a poor, coarse cloth; ironically, Dryden himself is said to have worn it in his early days in London. 'I remember plain John Dryden (before he paid his court with success to the great) in one uniform clothing of Norwich drugget.' *Gentleman's Magazine*, xv. 99 (February 1745).

35–6. Shadwell was reputed to be a musician and claimed the patronage of the King of Portugal.

42. *Epsom blankets:* Sir Samuel Hearty, a character in Shadwell's *The Virtuoso* (1676), is tossed in blankets.

43. *Arion:* legendary Greek musician who was saved from pirates on the back of a dolphin whom he charmed by his song.

a light within him; and writes by an inspiration which . . . a man must have no sense of his own when he receives.'

419. *faggoted his notions:* i.e. he made his verses out of disjointed single ideas. According to *Notes and Observations*, Settle 'has a Lottery of words by him, and draws them that come next, let them make sense or non-sense when they come together he matters not what'.

429. *For almonds he'll cry 'Whore':* Cf. Shakespeare, *Troilus and Cressida*, V. ii. 194–5: 'the parrot will not do more for an almond, than he for a commodious drab.'

430. *King David's brother:* In Settle's satire *Absalom Senior*, Absalom is the Duke of York.

437. *buggery:* in the context, bestiality: the allusion is to an obscene lampoon of the time.

444. *to write verse with him is to transprose:* the joke goes back to one against Dryden himself in Buckingham's *The Rehearsal* where Bayes (Dryden) describes his 'rule of transversion' for changing verse into prose or prose into verse.

446. Quoted from the opening lines of Settle's *Absalom Senior*.

451. *In fire-works:* Settle had been responsible for organizing celebrations dear to the Whigs, like those associated with 5 November.

454. *a puppet-show:* Settle is reputed to have written 'drolls' or puppet-plays for Southwark and Bartholomew fairs.

452. *serpents:* brings together in a pun satire which stings like a serpent and the firework of that name.

459. *Og:* Thomas Shadwell: after ridiculing him as a writer and dramatist in *Macflecknoe*, Dryden now satirizes Shadwell as a party writer for the Whigs. But his method is again that of a personal lampoon, expressing good-humoured contempt for Shadwell's girth and drinking habits. He takes the same approach in a prose pamphlet about this time: '*Og* may write against the King if he pleases, so long as he *Drinks* for him; and his *Writings* will never do the Government so much *harm*, as his *Drinking* does it *good*: for true Subjects will not much be perverted by his *Libels*; but the Wine *Duties* rise considerably by his *Claret*.'

461. *link:* the torch of pitch and tow carried by a link-boy.

494–5. The syntax is compressed: If Doeg be compared to you, your descriptions are so crude that even he may be called a poet, though an inferior one.

82. *Extract from* RELIGIO LAICI, *or* A LAYMAN'S FAITH

In this poem Dryden's sceptical, inquiring turn of mind has full play, as he thinks out aloud the religious problems that engage him in common with other men of the age. The occasion of the poem was the publication of Henry Dickinson's translation of Father Simon's *Histoire critique du*

144

47–8. *Pissing Alley . . . Aston Hall . . . :* sordid localities in London; the line is a typical instance of mock heroic bathos.

53–4. *St André . . . Psyche:* St André, a famous French dancing master, came over to be *maître de ballet* for Shadwell's opera *Psyche* in 1675.

55. I.e. the sentiments are exaggerated and the lines have too many syllables.

57–9. *Singleton . . . Villerius:* John Singleton (d. 1686) was one of the King's musicians. Villerius is a character in Davenant's opera *The Siege of Rhodes*.

64–78. This passage is modelled on the description of the cave of the winds in Cowley's *Davideis*, Book i.

64–5. *Augusta . . . much to fears inclined:* London, predominantly Whig, and therefore inclined to believe the wild rumours of the Popish Plot.

72–3. Mock-heroic parody of Cowley, *Davideis*, i:

> Where their vast *Court* the Mother-Waters keep,
> And undisturb'd by *Moons* in silence sleep.

74. *a Nursery:* a school for young actors.

78. *little Maximins:* Maximin is a ranting tyrant in Dryden's play *Tyrannick Love* (1670).

79–80. *buskins . . . socks:* the footwear of the actors in ancient tragedy and comedy respectively.

81; 84. *Simkin . . . Panton:* apparently characters in low farces.

90–3. Allusions to earlier plays by Shadwell.

101. *Martyrs of Pies:* the sheets of their books have been used to cover pies.

102. *Ogleby:* a voluminous hack-writer, cartographer-royal, and translator of Virgil (1649) and Homer (1660–5).

104. *Bilk'd stationers:* publishers ruined by the failure of their authors.

105. *Herringman:* Dryden's publisher until 1678, and publisher of Shadwell's plays.

106–11. Shadwell is compared to Ascanius, the son of Rome's legendary founder Aeneas; the passage is a parody of Virgil, *Aeneid*, ii. 682–4.

112. *As Hannibal:* Hannibal as a child was compelled by his father to swear eternal hatred to Rome (Livy, *History*, xxi. 1).

120. *sinister hand:* the sovereign carries the coronation orb in the left hand.

122. *Love's Kingdom:* pastoral play by Flecknoe (1664).

126. *poppies:* the poppy is a soporific and aphrodisiac; also, Shadwell is said to have been an opium addict.

129. *owls:* the owl signifies pedantic stupidity.

134–8. Shadwell is represented as possessed by the god of dullness who speaks through him as Apollo was supposed to speak through his prophetess.

141

139–40. Ireland signifies stupidity, and it was to Barbadoes that criminals were transported.

151. *gentle George:* Sir George Etherege (1634?–91?), Restoration comic dramatist; the following lines contain allusions to characters in his plays.

163. *S—dl—y:* Sir Charles Sedley, wit, dramatist, and friend of Dryden, had written a prologue for Shadwell's *Epsom-Wells* (1673).

168. *Sir Formal:* a bombastic character in Shadwell's *The Virtuoso.*

170. *Northern dedications:* Shadwell frequently dedicated his plays to the Duke or Duchess of Newcastle.

181. *sell bargains:* to give coarse replies to innocent questions.

184. There is some resemblance of plot between *Epsom-Wells* and Etherege's *She Would If She Could*, but Shadwell is not guilty of whole-sale plagiarism.

194. *tympany:* a flatulence that swells the body.

196. *kilderkin:* the fourth part of a tun.

204 ff. *iambic . . . anagram:* iambic metre was in Greek poetry originally the vehicle for satire. Anagrams, acrostics, and poems in shapes were rejected by the new school of poets; l. 207 may specifically refer to George Herbert's 'Easter Wings' and 'The Altar'.

212. In *The Virtuoso* Bruce and Longvil release a trap door under Sir Formal in the middle of his speech.

214–17. Like Elijah, Flecknoe bequeaths his mantle to Shadwell, his successor, but the whirlwind carries him not into heaven but down to hell. (2 Kings ii, 9–13).

76. *Extract from* ABSALOM AND ACHITOPHEL, PART TWO

This sequel, which carries the account of the Exclusion Bill crisis a stage further, was published in November 1682. The greater part of the poem is by Nahum Tate (1652–1715) writing under Dryden's direction; he has imitated the catalogue of the King's Whig and Nonconformist enemies in Part One; but ll. 310–509 which are given here are entirely by Dryden. The rich, burlesque study of Og recalls the earlier attack on Shadwell in *Macflecknoe.* As Scott says: 'Such pungent satire is easily distinguished from the smooth insipid flow of other parts, in which Dryden's corrections probably left nothing for censure, and which Tate was unable to qualify with any thing entitled to praise.'

312–13. *the tribe . . . in former sequestrations . . . :* those who had served the Parliamentary cause in the Civil War and profited from the confiscations or 'sequestrations' of Royalist property.

321. *Judas:* Robert Ferguson (d. 1714), a Scot, and therefore a 'false Hebronite'. He was ejected from his ministry under the Act of Uniformity in 1662; 'a hot and bold man . . . he had the management of a secret press,

and of a purse that maintained it' (Burnet, *History of His Own Time*, i. 542). He wrote pamphlets for Shaftesbury's party and was engaged in the plans for assassinating the King which culminated in the Rye House Plot of 1683.

325. *His college:* Ferguson directed a Nonconformist school at Islington.

330. *Phaleg:* James Forbes, a Scot, appointed tutor by the Duke of Ormonde to the Earl of Derby, husband of his granddaughter; there is, however, no justification for the slander in ll. 338–9.

335. *that buzzing insect:* refers to La Fontaine's fable 'Le Coche et la Mouche' (*Fables* vii. 9) in which a fly buzzing round the horses pretends that it has caused the coach to complete its journey.

338. *Can dry bones live?:* Ezek. xxxvii. 3.

353. *Ben-Jochanan:* Samuel Johnson (1649–1703): chaplain to the Whig Lord Russell, he had maintained the doctrine of popular sovereignt against that of passive obedience.

384. *the drunken patriarch:* Noah (Gen. ix. 18–27).

392. *thy hot father:* St Gregory of Nazianzus, whose attack on the emperor Julian had been invoked by Johnson. The sense of ll. 390–3 is: From your description of the heathen emperor (Julian the Apostate who attempted to revive the pagan gods) it appears that the apostate was the better man and the saint was not a true Father of the Church, but only of a sect.

396. *Balack:* Gilbert Burnet (1643–1715), later eminent as bishop an historian after the Revolution. He was out of favour for his Whig syn pathies in this period.

403. *David's psalms translated:* the metrical version of the Psalms Sternold and Hopkins, not noted for its poetic qualities.

405. *lame Mephibosheth the wizard's son:* Samuel Pordage (1633–91), son an astrologer. 2 Sam. iv. 4.

407. *rotten Uzza:* not certainly identified, but the Key of 1716 gi 'J.H.', and Kinsley suggests that he may be John How, whom Macau called 'the most rancorous and unprincipled of the Whigs'.

412. *Doeg:* Elkanah Settle (1648–1724), whose most celebrated play *The Empress of Morocco* (1673), was at one time a serious rival to Dry as a popular dramatist. He was at this time in the pay of Shaftesbury had violently attacked Dryden in *Absalom Senior: or, Achitophel Transp* (published in April 1682). Settle had a reputation for timidity (he refused a challenge to a duel) and therefore Dryden chooses the Doeg, of the Edomite traitor in 1 Sam. xxi–xxii., which means in He 'fearful', 'uneasy'.

415–17. *Through sense and nonsense*, etc. As in *Macflecknoe* the sa directed against loose or bombastic writing which lays claim to natural genius as a substitute for good sense. In *Notes and Observat The Empress of Morocco* (1674) to which Dryden contributed it is sa Settle '. . . would perswade us he is a kind of Phanatick in Poetry, *

vieux testament (1682). The book caused a stir among Anglicans because of its argument that since the manuscripts and the various translations of Scripture were unreliable, a rule of faith could not be based on the Bible alone. The implication was that the unquestioned authority of a Church was necessary for interpretation. Dryden was impressed by the work and its exposure of the limitations of human reason; as in the political poems he advocates a cautious compromise between private judgment and what must be taken on authority, but it is apparent that for him the inquiry is not over and that the Church of England has only his provisional allegiance.

Here Dryden abandons the elevated and figurative language of heroic poetry (employed to a limited extent in *Absalom and Achitophel*) for the tone of natural argument, supple and hesitating. As he says in the preface, 'A Man is to be cheated into Passion, but to be reason'd into Truth'.

1-11. The slow movement of the verse and gradual development of the simile admirably represent the tentative, exploratory character of the thought.

18. *interfering:* colliding. The reference is to the atomic theory of Epicurus, and that in the previous line is to Aristotle's doctrine of the unmoved mover, the deity who directs the universe from outside it.

21. *the Stagirite:* Aristotle, who was born at Stagira in Thrace.

42. *the Deist:* one who believes in a supreme and good being capable of acknowledgment by all men, but who does not accept the Christian revelation.

43. *Εὕρεκα:* Dryden's mistake for εὕρηκα, 'I have found it'. the exclamation of Archimedes when he discovered the method of determining the specific gravity of metals.

66-7. Dryden thinks, as he says in the preface, that the ideas of revealed religion faintly survived in the posterity of Noah and provided the source for the so-called 'natural religion' which is implanted in the minds of all mankind: 'So that we have not lifted up our selves to God, by the weak Pinions of our Reason, but he has been pleased to descend to us: and what *Socrates* said of him, what *Plato* writ, . . . is all no more than the Twilight of Revelation, after the Sun of it was set in the Race of *Noah*'. *Poems*, ed. Kinsley (Oxford, 1958), i. 304.

49. Inversion of subject and object.

69. *sprung:* Matt. iv. 16: 'to them which sat in the region and shadow of death light is sprung up'.

75. *renown'd* is transitive, and there is an inversion of subject and object: 'oracles proclaimed his wisdom'.

76-7. Cf. *Tyrannick Love* (1670), iv. 1:

> Thus with short plummets heav'ns deep will we sound,
> That vast abyss where humane wit is drown'd.

79. *Plutarch, Seneca, or Cicero?:* these writers are selected because their philosophical and moral writings were widely read and respected in post-Renaissance Europe.

86. Referring to the sacrifices of sheep, oxen, etc., in Greek and Roman religion.

128. *lustrations:* religious rites of purification.

140-1. The authors of the various parts of the Bible.

87. TO THE MEMORY OF MR OLDHAM

John Oldham (1653–83), an accomplished and fluent poet, was twenty years Dryden's junior though he preceded him as a satirist (cf. l. 8); he made his reputation by his satires on the Jesuits written during the Plot scare of 1679.

9. *Nisus:* see *Aeneid*, v. 328.

14. *numbers:* the special, polished form of the heroic couplet is meant, which Dryden himself mastered late.

23. *Marcellus:* the nephew of Augustus who died in his twentieth year, celebrated by Virgil, *Aeneid*, vi. 855.

88. A NEW SONG

Published in *Sylvae* (1685).

13. *die:* a common *double-entendre*, referring to the sexual climax.

14. *Trimmer:* name for a politician who tried to mediate between the two extremes of Whig and Tory (metaphor from sailing); Halifax was the chief Trimmer.

89. TO MRS ANNE KILLIGREW

Anne Killigrew, maid of honour to Mary of Modena, the queen of James II, died of smallpox in 1685. This ode appeared in the volume of her poems published after her death. Johnson calls it 'the noblest ode that our language ever has produced', and E. M. W. Tillyard has recently agreed with this verdict, though some modern critics have been unable to stomach the formal splendour of its apostrophes and allusions.

6-11. I.e. whether you have been translated to the planets, or to the stars beyond (thought by the old astronomy to be fixed), or be an angel (seraph) in the presence of God.

23. *traduction:* according to the doctrine called traducianism the soul of man is not created at birth but transmitted from his parents.

26. *Thy father:* Henry Killigrew, poet and dramatist.

29-33. *pre-existing soul*, etc.: alluding to the Pythagorean doctrine of the transmigration of souls: the soul passes from one body to another to attain purification.

33. *Sappho:* Greek woman poet.

43. *in trine:* in astrology planets separated by 120 degrees in the zodiac have a fortunate influence on births or events. The survival of a horoscope cast for his son suggests that Dryden took astrology seriously.

49. *no clust'ring swarm:* there was a fable that bees settled on the lips of the infant Plato as a presage of his eloquence.

65. *steaming ordures of the stage:* in referring to the licentiousness of the contemporary stage Dryden must be aware of his own considerable contribution to it.

82. *Epictetus with his lamp:* Dryden confuses Epictetus with Diogenes, who went about with a lantern in daytime saying: 'I am looking for an honest man'.

87. *Diana:* goddess of chastity.

88. *the Nine:* the Muses.

134. *our phoenix queen:* uniquely beautiful, like the fabulous phoenix, of which there exists only one specimen at a time. The queen is Mary of Modena.

162. *Orinda:* the name given in the literary world to the poetess Katherine Philips, who also died of smallpox.

165. *her warlike brother:* Henry Killigrew, a naval captain, at this time absent in the Mediterranean.

180. *the valley of Jehosaphat:* Joel iii. 2.

96. Extracts from THE HIND AND THE PANTHER

Dryden began to attend mass early in 1686 but it is not known exactly when he was received into the Roman Catholic Church.

The Hind and the Panther is a statement of his faith and an attempt to reconcile his former friends in the Anglican High Church party to the position he had now reached. If the poem is gentle in its treatment of the noble Panther, the Church of England, it is harsh, as Dryden consistently was, towards the Protestant Dissenters. James II had begun his reign with a policy conforming to these sentiments, but by the time that the poem was published (April 1687) he had issued a Declaration of Indulgence to conciliate the Dissenters and win them over to his side. This was anathema to the Anglicans. Dryden did something to correct the political anachronism of the poem in a prose preface which he wrote for it. It is, in fact, not a poem on the Tory party line like *Absalom and Achitophel* and *The Medal*, but a moving and sincere statement of his individual progress from scepticism to belief. It is also the nearest approach Dryden made to the form of the heroic poem to which he so aspired. In its mixture of styles, the grand and the familiar, as in the fantasy of the beast-fable, it preserves something of Elizabethan richness. On its position as the climax of Dryden's poetic achievement, and on the manner in which it concludes the sceptical quest of *Religio Laici*, see F. T. Prince, 'Dryden Redivivus', *Review of English Literature* (1960) i. 71–9.

1. *Hind:* the Catholic Church.

8. *doomed . . . fated:* 'Doomed', condemned: sentenced to death by an earthly court but not destined to perish.

14. *Caledonian:* British, not Scottish. Dryden uses the classical device of using the part for the whole.

35. *the bloody Bear:* the Independents or Congregationalists, described as destructive of form and ceremony.

37. *the quaking Hare:* the Quakers, described as timid and introspective.

39. *the buffoon Ape:* the free-thinkers.

41. *the Lion:* James II.

43. *the bristl'd Baptist Boar:* the enemies of the Baptists reproached them with the fanaticism and excesses of the sect under John of Leyden which seized Munster in 1521.

53. *False Reynard:* the Arians or Socinians, who denied the divinity of the second person of the Trinity.

54–5. *Athanasius . . . Nice:* Athanasius contested the Arian doctrines at the Council of Nice, and the creed bearing his name is a statement of orthodox Trinitarianism.

72 ff. A rare and vivid passage of autobiographical confession.

95. *Impassible:* incapable of suffering injury.

327. *The Panther:* the Anglican Church, symbolized as beautiful but dangerous.

342. *spirits of a middle sort:* Milton describes 'Spirits Betwixt th' Angelical and Human kind', *Paradise Lost*, iii. 461–2.

537. *The ten-horn'd monster:* Protestants thought that the monster of Rev. xvii. prophesied the Roman Church.

552. *the Hind had seen him first:* in beast lore, a wolf can make other animals dumb if he sees them first.

563. *fellow-suff'rer in the plot:* Anglicans during the Popish Plot were accused of being crypto-Papists.

ii. 1281. *of the Stygian race:* Hercules, nephew of Pluto, who overcame the three-headed dog Cerberus, guardian of hell, and is therefore compared to Christ who led the souls out of captivity.

1283. *Pan:* Christ, God of shepherds who died for his sheep; the parallel is common in the religious pastoral poetry of the Renaissance.

iii. 1721 ff. The fable of the Swallows, said by Dryden in his preface to be 'a distinct story by itself', is a masterpiece of easy, rapid narrative. The swallows are the Catholics, prosperous under the rule of James II but rightly fearing that the rashness of official policy (the delay of their winter flight) will cause a renewal of persecution. The Martin is Father Petre, James II's confessor.

1750. *a mack'rel gale:* mackerel are caught when a fresh breeze is blowing.

1894. *Virgin Balance:* the sun passes from the zodiacal sign of Virgo (the Virgin) into Libra (the Balance) on 21 September.

1905. *dorp:* village; a Dutch word cognate with English *thorpe*.

1908. *Sick-feather'd:* with young, weak feathers.

1925. *poll'd 'em down:* struck them down with poles, or perhaps simply, lopped them off the top of the trees.

1927. *the laws provide:* under a law of Elizabeth it was high treason for Catholic priests or Jesuits to remain in England.

1932. *change of winds:* the body of the kingfisher, if hung by the bill, is supposed to show in which direction the wind is. Sir Thomas Browne, *Vulgar Errors*, iii. x.

106. A SONG FOR ST CECILIA'S DAY, 1687

Written for a musical society which from 1683 onwards had annually commissioned a poet and a composer to provide a choral ode for this occasion (22 November). Ten years later Dryden contributed another ode, *Alexander's Feast*.

The ode is written in the 'Pindarick' or irregular manner with dissimilar stanza patterns.

1-2. *From harmony ... this universal frame began:* a Platonic idea for which Dryden may be indebted to Milton's 'At a Solemn Music'.

8. *cold, and hot, and moist, and dry:* the elements of which the universe is composed according to the ancient cosmology; cf. *Paradise Lost*, iii. 708–15.

15. *diapason:* the whole range of notes in the scale.

17. *Jubal* 'the father of all such as handle the harp and organ' (Gen. iv. 21).

52. *organ:* the association with organ music is a late development of the legend. In the medieval story St Cecilia was visited on earth by a guardian angel; Dryden transforms the angel into a spirit of harmony.

50. *Sequacious:* inclined to follow, a Latinism.

61–3. *The trumpet:* cf. Isa. xxvii. 13; 1 Cor. xv. 52.

63. *untune:* when the physical world comes to an end at the Last Judgment the music of the spheres will cease.

109. *Epilogue to* KING ARTHUR

The opera *King Arthur* was written for Charles II but not performed till 1691.

Mrs Bracegirdle: a famous and attractive actress.

2. *Bow Street:* then a fashionable district.

17. *Bridges Street:* notorious at this period for its brothels.

31. *your face shall be my sign:* when the haberdasher has his own shop he will put up her picture outside as his trade sign.

III. THE LADY'S SONG

This is a Jacobite song, hinting at 'the banishment of King James and his beautiful consort Mary of Este' (Scott).

112. *Epilogue to* HENRY THE SECOND

5. *Rosamond:* Fair Rosamond who in the play dies after being given poison by Queen Eleanor.

20. *Haynes:* an actor who turned Catholic under James II and Protestant again under William III.

22. *chapels of ease:* were built in outlying districts for the convenience of parishioners who could not get to church.

114. TO MY DEAR FRIEND MR CONGREVE ON HIS COMEDY CALL'D THE DOUBLE-DEALER

Dryden, always ready to encourage youthful talent, wrote this epistle for the second play by the twenty-three-year-old William Congreve (1694) which had not been so successful with the public as his first, *The Old Bachelor*. The epistle contains a critical review of the literature of his own age.

2. *wit:* creative intelligence and power.

7–8. *Like Janus . . . :* the god Janus was supposed to have introduced the arts of agriculture into Italy.

14. *second temple:* the Jewish temple rebuilt after the return from exile in Babylon.

15. *Vitruvius:* Roman writer on architecture.

29. *Southerne:* Thomas Southerne, dramatist (1660–1746).

30. *Manly Wycherley:* William Wycherley (1640–1715), author of *The Plain Dealer* and *The Country Wife*, stands with Etherege and Congreve in the forefront of the Restoration comic dramatists. He is called Manly in allusion to the hero of *The Plain Dealer*.

35. *Fabius:* Scipio, the Roman general against the Carthaginians, was elected consul when below the official age, though jealously opposed by Fabius. Dryden means that if Scipio had possessed the charm of Congreve, Fabius would have had no cause to be jealous.

39. *old Romano:* Dryden is confused here: Giulio Romano was the pupil of Raphael, not his master.

41–8. Dryden lost his offices of Poet Laureate and Historiographer-Royal at the Revolution. They were given respectively to his old rival Thomas

Shadwell ('Tom the first') and Thomas Rymer ('Tom the second'). 'my patron' (l. 49) is Dryden's friend the Earl of Dorset who had to carry out his official functions in distributing these offices. But he had helped Dryden privately.

63. *she:* perhaps used instead of 'it' because in an earlier draft Dryden had 'Nature' for 'heaven', and has not troubled to complete his revision.

67. *th' ungrateful stage:* Dryden's final plays had little success; he had just completed the last of them, *Love Triumphant* (published in 1695).

64. *post:* position.

65. *proceed:* progress.

72. *Be kind to my remains:* in 1717 Congreve edited Dryden's plays with a splendid tribute.

116. *Extract from* THE AENEID OF VIRGIL

Dryden was a skilful and prolific translator. His principal achievement was *The Works of Virgil, Translated into English Verse* (1697), the major task of his poetic life. It took him four years to complete and was published by subscription in a sumptuous folio by Tonson. In addition to this he produced *The Satires of Juvenal and Persius made English* (1693) with a long discourse on the nature of satire, and many versions of Ovid, Horace and Lucretius in the collection *Examen Poeticum* and the earlier *Sylvae* (1685). Dryden's method of translation is bold and free, assimilating both the language and the mode of thought of the classics to those of the English Augustan age, and to those standards for a diction worthy of heroic poetry which he and other critics had worked out. He thus laid the foundations of the formal 'poetic diction' of the eighteenth century.

Dido and Aeneas, Book iv. ll. 181-246. Aeneas, on his way to accomplish his destined task of re-establishing the Trojan state in Italy, is given shelter by Dido, queen of Carthage; this passage describes the hunt which is dispersed by a storm; Dido and Aeneas, already fatally attracted, seek shelter in the same cave and become lovers. Subsequently Aeneas abandons Dido to fulfil his mission and she takes her own life.

198. *a golden caul:* a sort of cap (an archaism).

118. TO MY HONOUR'D KINSMAN, JOHN DRIDEN

Dryden uses both spellings of his family name indifferently. This John Driden was his cousin, a Whig country gentleman and M.P., but an opponent of the war policy of William III. He showed great kindness to Dryden in his last years. The poem was included in the *Fables* and its author thought it the best in the book.

1 ff. *How blest:* the idealization of the country life is a frequent theme in Augustan poetry, as in that of the Roman poets they imitated, particu-

larly Horace. The sentiments correspond to a reality: the solid social basis of the squirearchy and the balance of town and country.

43. *Rebecca's heir:* John Driden's estate had come to him through his mother.

46. *Ceres:* goddess of agriculture and the harvest.

51. *champian:* open country, usually a noun but here an adjective.

72. *weekly bill:* the weekly bill of mortality showing the number of those who had died within the cities of London and Westminster.

75. *Pity:* 'it is a pity that.'

80. *vindicates:* claims its revenge on.

82. *Gibbons:* Dryden's physician.

83-5. *Maurus:* Sir Richard Blackmore (1655-1729), another physician, had murdered Maro's (Virgil's) Muse by writing a bad epic poem, *Prince Arthur* (1695).

87. *M—lb—rne:* Luke Milbourne, a clergyman who had attacked Dryden's translation of Virgil.

107. *Garth:* Sir Samuel Garth (1661-1719), wit and physician, maintained a free dispensary for the poor which caused a selfish outcry by the apothecaries; the dispute is the subject of his humorous poem *The Dispensary*.

140. *Munster:* the Bishop of Munster had supported England against Holland in return for subsidies, but had proved a doubtful ally.

142. *peace:* the Treaty of Ryswick had brought to an end William III's war against France, which had become unpopular.

152. *Namur:* William's capture of Namur in 1695 had hastened the peace.

188. *your gen'rous grandsire:* Sir Erasmus Driden, their grandfather, one of those sent to prison on the eve of Charles I's third parliament (1628) on account of the loan money.

125. *Extract from* THE COCK AND THE FOX

Dryden's last collection of poems, the *Fables Ancient and Modern* (1700), is remarkable for its mellow serenity and for the evidence it gives of his mastery of the art of telling a story in verse. It consists of adaptations from Chaucer and Boccaccio.

In the Preface to the *Fables*, as well as the praise of Chaucer quoted in in the Introduction (pp. 13-14), Dryden gives the following defence of the liberties he has taken in adapting Chaucer into modern English:

Words are not like Landmarks, so sacred as never to be remov'd: Customs are chang'd, and even Statutes are silently repeal'd, when the Reason ceases for which they were enacted. As for the other Part of the Argument, that his Thoughts will lose of their original Beauty, by the innovation of Words; in the first place, not only their Beauty, but their Being is lost, where they are no longer understood, which is the present Case. I grant, that something must be lost in all Transfusion, that is, in all Translations; but the Sense will remain, which would otherwise be lost, or at least be maim'd, when it is scarce intelligible, and that but to a few. How few are there who can read *Chaucer*, so as to understand him perfectly? And if imperfectly, then with less Profit, and no Pleasure. 'Tis not for the Use of some old *Saxon* Friends, that I have taken these Pains with him . . . but for their sakes who understand Sense and Poetry as well as they; when that Sense and Poetry is put into Words which they understand.

126. THE SECULAR MASQUE

The Secular Masque was written to be performed with *The Pilgrim*, a play by Fletcher revived for Dryden's benefit during the last month of his life. It may well be his last composition.

'By the introduction of the deities of the chace, of war, and of love, as governing the various changes of the seventeenth century, the poet alludes to the sylvan sports of James the First, the bloody wars of his son, and the licentious gallantry which reigned in the courts of Charles II and James' (Scott). But the symbolism is a mellow comment on life in general as the poet had experienced it, his 'ripeness is all', and need not be interpreted with such exclusive attention to history.

INDEX OF TITLES AND FIRST LINES

155